Tribal Philosophy

Tribal Philosophy

SANTOSH KIRO

PRABHAT
PAPERBACKS

Published by
PRABHAT PAPERBACKS
An imprint of Prabhat Prakashan Pvt. Ltd.
4/19 Asaf Ali Road,
New Delhi-110002 (INDIA)
e-mail: prabhatbooks@gmail.com

ISBN 978-93-5521-123-1
TRIBAL PHILOSOPHY
by Santosh Kiro

Edition
First, 2022

Price
₹ 350 (Rupees Three Hundred Fifty Only)

Printed at
Sanjay Printers, Sahibabad

To My Father Sohrai and Mother Flora

Foreword

As a student of Philosophy, having keen interest in Adivasi philosophy, I was very delighted when Dr. Santosh Kiro requested me to write the foreword of his forthcoming monograph. Somebody venturing into, what he terms as 'Tribal Philosophy', was a matter of pleasant surprise for me. A scholar endeavouring to philosophise tribal life seemed surprising particularly because of the fact that there has not been very honest and persistent effort in studying this important aspect of this community by the students of Philosophy. So tribal, more so Adivasi studies, have virtually remained so far, the favourite domain of the sociologists, anthropologists, historians, and lately of political scientists. In this sense, Dr. Kiro's work is more or less treading a lone furrow. For me, this internal reading of a community is very encouraging at a time when Adivasi studies have been dominated by non-Adivasi scholars.

However, at the outset, I would like to caution all those scholars who are expecting another philosophical work laden with foot and end notes, a long bibliography and theorisations. Dr. Kiro has avoided this academic mold. Instead, he has chosen the simple way of presenting his facts and ideas in lucid language in order to produce a substantive text. The information culled has also been suitably analysed to serve the purpose of philosophisation. I am deeply impressed when the author makes an intelligent blend of textual and empirical methodologies. In this way, he has been able to carve a novel way of constructing philosophical texts. In doing this, Dr. Kiro has retrieved and examined a large body of Adivasi folklore as depicted by Srijan Kani and Asur Kani in particular.

To collect and use folklore as a staple has been the most appropriate method when there is a deplorable dearth of literature on Adivasi philosophy. I have no hesitation in saying that this has helped the author to attribute the exact meanings of many cultural codes practised in the Adivasi world and about which the mainstream society has not been very sensitive. This intervention has therefore been long awaited. I shall particularly draw attention to one core idea that constitutes the entire ensemble of Adivasi worldview. Scholars who have so far drawn on Sociological, Anthropological and Historical literature are aware of their writings on Adivasi identity assertion and their notion of being and belonging; Adivasi notion of an egalitarian and homogenous social order; community governance and aesthetics. In his The Making of a Village: The Dynamics of Adivasi Rural Life in India (Routledge 2021), Dr. Asoka Kumar Sen elaborates how Adivasi notions of self and governance have been anchored on their novel idea of 'moral society' and seeks to portray what this moral society has been. Dr. Kiro should be given the credit of exploring and foregrounding the ontological notion of this moral social order that pivoted Adivasi sense of being. Furthermore, the author helps correct some prevailing misconceptions about the Adivasi world. One such concept the work has been able to modify is the idea that Adivasis are animists.

The work impressed me more so for its comparative philosophical approach where Dr. Kiro has brought Hinduism, Christianity and Adivasi worldview on board. He has elaborated how Hindu and Adivasi world have drawn on each other and how Adivasi society is indebted to Christianity. This comparative approach has enabled the author to show that humankind has not been completely insulated and compartmentalised. Through centuries there have been meetings of cultures, reciprocity and exchange of ideas. Despite acculturation, Dr. Kiro has commendably showed to what extent Adivasi communities could maintain their individuality and distinction.

I expect this commendable work will be widely circulated and acclaimed by scholars across disciplines. More so, this venture will inspire other Adivasi intellectuals to come forward to enrich this new genre of philosophical literature.

–Padmaja Sen

Former Professor and Head,

Department of Philosophy & Dean, Humanities

Kolhan University, Chaibasa

Author's Note

If the thought processes of the world are to be categorised on the basis of Myths of Creation, there are only two broad categories. First, the Creation sprang ex-nihilo (out of nothing) and second, the Creation came 'out of something'—the 'something' being the primordial things or the Panchatatva according to Eastern lexicon. Individuals, completely oblivious of the by-products of these two sets of thought or about these two thoughts themselves, live and die according to beliefs and norms that either of these two sets of thoughts tacitly set for them.

The ex-nihilo thought says that there existed nothing except the Supreme Spirit or Supreme Mind in the beginning and this Spirit or Mind caused everything into being. Thus, 'matter' came from 'spirit'. In normal course of action, like begets the likes but here 'like' begets the 'unlikes'—mind creates matter.

The ex-nihilo school is adhered to mostly by the West, who believe that matter has to be created and mind can create it. Matter enters the world at some point of time—after it is created by the mind. The 'out of something' set of thought, adhered to mostly by the East, believes that matter 'has been there' since the beginning, and that it does not need to be created. Role of the mind is completely absent here. These two sets of school entirely module the thought process of the people who unconsciously submit to the school of the region they are in. While the ex-nihilo goes on creating, because creation is in its very nature as things do not exist from the beginning and they have to be created, for the 'out of something' people, things existed since the very beginning—'it was/is there'.

For the ex-nihilo school, matter is subject to mind, and since mind is the creator of matter, mind is the master of matter, say, the world. Here is the root to the ills that plaugue the world today. If this school is let a loose run for ever, it is set to spell doom for the world eventually. On the other hand, the 'out of something' school does not inspire mind (man) to work for anything new—new invention, discovery, research etc, as 'this thing was there' since the beginning of time.

There is yet another angle to the Myth of Creation—sex. Going by the Western school, woman was created for man as he felt lonely living alone, taking a few parts from his body. Even the Eastern school has a similar thought—that man felt lonely living alone and hence divided himself into two. So in both the West and the East, man and woman have a natural instinct to become one again. In the Tribal school of thought, however, woman is not part of man, for the two were born simultaneously from two eggs. And that sexual union had to be taught by the one who created them. In both the cases, gender inequality or equality is just a corollary.

Nature is a favourite subject of national and international deliberations in recent days. In the ex-nihilo school, Spirit placed Nature at the foot of the man and declared him as the 'master'. Now, the master can do any thing with the Nature. And the master is actually doing anything—result is all there for everyone to see. The 'out of something' school is literally thoughtless on this point. But the Tribal school of thought is clear—that man is part of Nature and since he is bestowed with intellect, he has to act as the elder brother who protects and cares.

It is alleged that philosophy does not bake a cake. In fact, it doesn't, because there are other disciplines to do so. But philosophy sets thoughts like: What is bread? Why would man need bread at all? If he has to need bread to remain alive, why would he remain alive at all? And so on. Thus, philosophy sets the entire rule of the game called life. From 'may his soul rest in peace' to 'Ram naam satya hai', all of it is rule set by philosophy through and through.

Away from the East or the West—'out of something' or 'out of nothing' schools of thoughts, there are some distinctively set apart thought-worlds. Tribal India's thought process is one such and it does not seem to adhere strictly to either of the two established set of thoughts, but in many ways present interesting views completely on its own. The Tribal World is both colourful and attractive, in that there is immense depth for intellectual immersion. The world has only seen the outer walls of Tribal India painted with colourful culture and traditions. True discovery of the inner world of Tribal India is still awaited. The present work is an attempt at this.

Acknowledgements

I want to thank professors of Ranchi University, Department of Philsophy. Dr Sushil Ankan, Dr S.N. Jha, Dr Saraswati Mishra, Dr Usha Kiran and Dr Ajay Kumar Singh who helped me in various valuable ways in this work. I thank Dr Prakash Chandra Dubey, Former Head, Department of Philosophy, Veer Kunwar Singh University (Bihar), for his guidance. A part of my Ph.D. Thesis in which these great scholars guided me through, has been adapted and included in the present work.

My sincere thanks to Late Dr R.N. Sinha, Former Professor of English, and Dean of Humanities, St. Xavier's College, Ranchi (Autonomous), who paintskingly edited my work.

I express my gratitude to Basavi, Rajendra and Ashish, who helped me in multifarious ways in this work.

Acknowledgements

Contents

CHAPTER 1

The Undiscovered World

Elephant or Woman

A long time ago, there was a Munda couple that lived in the Munda *dishum* (country). When the only son of the Munda couple became an adult, the father found a beautiful young woman and got her married to the son. They were allotted a separate room in the house. The father-in-law had huge tracts of land, an equally large livestock and a large black dog *Kalu*. The dog would sleep near the door of the house and sincerely keep vigil during night.

One night, Kalu barked hard and the father woke up abruptly. He thought some stray cattle might have turned up in the courtyard and was making a noise, to which Kalu barked. He kept lying down on his bed, but with a vigilant ear to the sounds. After a while, Kalu stopped barking. But on the following night at the same hour, Kalu barked again. The father, however, thought that Kalu might again be barking habitually at some stray animal. On successive nights too, Kalu kept repeating his barks at the same hour of the night.

One night, Kalu barked too hard and the old man decided to get up from his bed and see for himself. He slowly came out of his room and tip-toed to the main door of his house. To his horror he saw a sight that frightened him to the core. He thought he had seen some bad dream. Or it was probably a hallucination. He went back to his bed and lay down trying to quieten his mind. The sight of that night would not go from the old man's mind and would keep coming back again and again even during the day. But he decided not to discuss it with anyone. Night came and at the same hour Kalu barked hard again. The old man gathered courage and walked to the door of the house. To his horror again, he saw the same sight. A woman had taken the form of a huge animal with her nose too long and legs like logs. Her ears had grown too big and they dangled in the air. She slowly turned herself into her original self and when she had completed changing form, the old man now clearly saw that she was his daughter-in-law. 'So, it's my daughter-in-law!' he told himself in complete disblelief. 'She converted herself into an animal and went out at night to roam about; and Kalu barked at her when she came back home to change her form again!' the old man had not doubt now. 'Stop there," he ordered in a rembling voice. And when she stood in front of him, he said with a voice sterner, "You have deceived me.

Adopt the form of the same animal and go away from my house. No longer shall I keep you in my house". The old man then called out his son who slept in the room snoring in complete ignorance of what was happening outside, and said, "Son, you have not bothered to keep knowledge of what your wife does. You too must leave my house at once and go with her".

From that night onwards, the daughter-in-law and the son left the house of the Munda. The daughter-in-law converted herself into that same animal and then converted her own husband too, and left for the forest. They became elephants and lived in the forest.

The young Munda couple, who were now an elephant couple, roamed about at night in the forests and forest-villages in search of food and water. On occasional instances, they went to the agriculture field of their father and ate, to their heart's content, paddy and other agricultural produces. The old Munda allowed them to have as much as they needed for their sustenance, but did not welcome them back home. All the elephants are now the descendants of this same young Munda couple. Their mother tongue is Mundari and they continue to converse among themselves in the same tongue. Whenever, they hear this tongue speak, they understand all the spoken words and obey what is being told to them.[1]

The Elephant Myth of the Mundas

*

India is a mysterious land, a boiling pot of numerous groups and their gods—the power of a god proportionate to the collective strength of the people who worship him. There is another India within this greater India—the 'Tribal India', where such stories as Elephant Myth abound. It is the unseen India, more mysterious than the *India* people know and have read. Indological works have thrown light only sparingly on this India, and if systematic works are undertaken, they may well form what can be termed as *Tribo-Indology within Indology*. A large number of Tribes residing in different parts of the sub-continent since ages, each with its distinctive language and culture, naturally create a very colourful *Tribal India*.

With its distinctive socio-religious practices, rites, rituals and belief systems which until now have been thinly understood by the mainstream society—if at all there is one; the Tribal World is still a mystery to many. Most men think that Tribal society does not have a philosophy, does not have a God (or gods), and does not have a worldview, does not explain meaning of life and human existence. All of this is absolutely incorrect and grossly wrong. On the contrary, the Tribal society in India has a well developed system that explains nearly every philosophical question: questions of life, death, existence and Creation. No man or society can exist without a philosophy—some men or society may have well-discussed, well-deliberated philosophy, while others may have a philosophy that has not been discussed or discussed well-enough, and hence remain restricted and limited to the society concerned. So far as the Tribal society in India is concerned, it is sad that not much attention has been paid to their philosophy and worldview. The Tribal society bristles with rich folktales, folklores, traditions, legends and myths—

all of which when analysed, bear the philosophical tenets that make up 'Tribal Philosophy'.

Tribal society in India, however, is diverse and heterogenous; each having its own kind of philosophy. The word 'Tribal' itself is without a boundary, and epistemologically it means every human group which has or had tribal character of living. The present work deals with the Munda Tribes (Austro-Asiatic Tribes). Just as any Philosophy would have to be drawn from myths, legends, social and religious practices and worldview, the Munda Tribes too offer ample scope for a philosophy to be drawn up from their rich folktales, folklores, myths and legends, social and religious practices and worldview.

The Munda group, one of the most prominent groups of Tribes in India, who live mostly in Central India, form a very interesting group for a philosophical study; and when their god, world, man and sex is compared with those in other philosophical traditions—Vedic and Christian, their philosophy can be understood in a better manner.

God or No God?

Often times, one comes across questions like: Does the Tribal society have a concept of God (gods)? Does it have a philosophy? The Munda Tribes too face these questions that usually come from the mainstream society and mainstream intellectuals. Because, what the mainstream ordinarily observes is the external worship system of the Tribal society: worshipping trees, hills and mountains—or Nature as a whole. They term the system as Animism and call the Mundas Animists—Nature worshippers.

The problem, however, is not so simple as it appears to the naked eye. If the Mundas are *only* Nature worshippers and Animists— restricting themselves to Animism—who then is *Singbonga*, who then are the *Bongas*? Singbonga and Bonga is a living tradition, and philosophers have very thinly dwelt upon this question.

In order to understand who Singbonga is and who the Bongas are, it is the Asur Kani (the Legend of the Asurs) that will throw light on the issue. This is not just a legend, but the 'unwritten traditional document on which the present system of religious feasts and rites observed by the Mundas is based'[2].

The Asur Kani

A *Kani* (legend) to the Mundas is what the *Puranas* are to the Vedic people. As the *Puranas* contain narratives about the history of the Universe from creation to destruction and the genealogies of kings, heroes, sages, and deities, so does a *Kani* narrates oral history, cosmology, geography, war and peace, usually written in the form of a dialogue. Gods and worldviews in India seem to have been constructed or de-constructed on a specific historical and geographical situation, particularly after a win or loss in battle for supremacy. Asur Kani too has a similar background. Historically, it talks more of a battle for supremacy between the Mundas and the Asur Tribes in which the Mundas succeeded. Ironically, the Asurs are the older branch of the Mundas. The poor Asurs were at the receiving end, both from the Mundas and the Vedic people!

The Asur Kani, in Brief, Goes Thus:

Singbonga, who created the universe, Nature, creatures and the man and woman, lived in *sirma* (heaven), with his golden sceptre ever dazzling.

Down below on the earth, the mighty Asurs smelted iron day in and day out, heating up the entire earth. The grass withered, tanks dried up, bulls and cows, and other creatures including men and women did not get food to eat and water to drink. They complained to Singbonga about it, pleading with Him to show Asurs the reason.

Singbonga summoned the Fearless King Crow and sent him to the Asurs as a messenger. 'Listen! I have brought you a message, I have come with a request,' the King Crow informed Asurs of the message of Singbonga. 'The creeping insects and the flying insects and birds do no longer find water and food. On earth the grasses and herbs, the trees and shrubs are withering. In heaven, Singbonga feels the heat and gets scorched.'

The Asurs caught hold of the King Crow and insulted him. He fled to save himself.

Singbonga then sent the Golden Vulture as His messenger. The Asurs did the same with him too. Singbonga sent many more messengers to the Asurs, but each time a messenger arrived from Singbonga, the Asurs insulted him and chased him away.

Finally, Singbonga, taking the form of an itch-covered boy descended upon the earth, and by craft destroyed the Asurs with the help of their own wives.

When Singbonga was going up to *sirma* (heaven), the Asur women caught hold of his legs and hands.

"After that He rises to heaven. And then those Asur women cling to His cloth. Then, He catching them by the topknots of their hair, threw them off. The one who fell on a hill became a *buru bonga* (a hill spirit); the one who fell into deep water became the *ikir bonga* (a spirit of the deep); the one who fell on high ground and near the head of a ravine became *nage bonga*; the one who fell on a high became a *karang buru bonga*; the one who fell on a wooden spot became *deasuli bonga*, the one who fell on a wooden spot near a spring became *chondor ikir bonga*; the one who fell on a pebble or round stone became *chandi bonga*."[3]

Singbonga: Who and What?

The Munda Legend of Creation—*Sirjan Kani* talks of how the Supreme Spirit, Singbonga, who was Self-Created, created the World. He of course had his wife since the beginning of time, and the Legend too mentions of her. The oral history of Munda *Srijan Kani* describes the nature and attributes of Singbonga, the Munda God.

Singbonga is a Creator God. But He is the Creator only in the sense that The *Primordial* elements are Eternal, just as Himself; and He used them to create. He creates the world, trees, herbs, animals and plants there on, but not the water and aquatic creatures. He did not create 'Earth'—a primordial element, but *found* it out with the help of aquatic creatures. Munda philosophy, thus, presupposes the existence of the Primordial elements like water, earth, wind, ether and fire.

Singbonga is also the Preserver God. In the Asur Legend, He listens to the complaints of the earth creatures, and trees and herbs, who were withering due to the excessive heat created by the iron-smelting of the Asurs. Singbonga also destroys. Singbonga, however, does not seem much identical to the concept of Trinity: Father, Son and the Holy Spirit in Christianity, who are different in Persons but at the same time One—as per the Christian idea of Unity of Godheads Though in Christianity too, there is the idea of Creator (God the Father or Yahweh of Judaism), Destroyer (God the Father or Yahweh of Judaism), Preserver (Holy Spirit) and Redeemer (Christ, the Son), in the Munda religious tradition, the same Singbonga plays all these roles.

But unlike the Hindu tradition of Incarnation of Gods in order to either preserve—like in case of Vishnu Avatara, Singbonga does not seem to take Incarnation so many times. He does so when he takes the 'human form' to do something quickly and returns to his abode soon— as revealed by the Asur Kani. Another time Singbonga took the human form is when He taught the first *boy and girl* how to have sex, narrated by the Mundas and other Munda Tribes alike, in the Legend of Procreation.

Singbonga is a complete Spirit with a power to adopt any form at will. Thus, though He is all Spirit, He can take different forms too, if He so wishes.

Bonga (Spirit) and Singbonga?

Mundas are often seen worshipping at hills (*buru*), rivers (*gara or ikir*), trees (*daru*) etc, on different occasions. The Asur legend gives ample explanation to this religious act of the Mundas. The Asur legend is an orally narrated traditional document on which the present system of religious feasts and rites observed by the Mundas, is based.

In the Asur legend, when Singbonga had destroyed the iron-smelting Asurs who worked ceaselessly and was going back to His abode in Heaven, the Asur women clung on to different parts of His body. They told Him: 'We did not think that Thou wouldst act in this manner. Thou hast made us burn our men to death.'—'What then?', He answered. 'I sent you the watchful shrike and the energetic king-crow as messengers. You did not obey their orders—this probably is the root incident why for the Munda Tribes messages come through birds and animals—usually called omen, and reading the omen and acting accordingly is important—and then He asked them: 'Will you obey my messages and commands?' 'Unless we obey, how can we possibly find our sustenance?'—'All right then, I shall show you a way whereby you will be supported,' He answered. 'Before going away I will establish a witch-finder with a disciple. These two will endeavour to find out in divination by means of broken rice, by means of the flame of a lamp or of a lighted flayed stem of the *Hibiscus cannabinus* or *Crotalaria junecia* plants. I order you not to hide yourselves from the witch-finder and his aide. In the middle of each village there will be a Munda public sacrificer who will offer you sacrifice under a tree.'[4]

At first sight, it appears that the Munda concept of God is solely Animism and Polytheism. Neither of it however is fully correct. Munda Tribe is not *just* Nature Worshipper. This Tribe worships only Singbonga, the Supreme Sprit, residing in *Sirma*—Heaven. The sacrifice, thus, in the Singbonga tradition, has to be made under a tree. This, to the bare eye, suggests that the Mundas are worshipping the tree. As per belief, Singbonga loves to come and rest on a *Shorea robusta* (Sal tree) whenever He is invoked upon by the Munda priest (*Pahan*), and the *pahan* has been instructed by Singbonga to worship and offer sacrifice at the foot of a tree, usually *Shorea robusta.*

Munda philosophy, thus, cannot conceive the existence of God in the absence of the Nature. God gets immanent in Nature and when Nature is worshipped, Singbonga himself is worshipped. The whole of Nature is the dwelling place of God, or in other words, the whole of Nature is the 'facial expression' of God, the Supreme Spirit. 'Any and everything that exists in the world is nothing more than a modification of the attributes of God'[5], and 'God (Singbonga) is the world and the world is in Him', He is the source of everything that is, and in this sense, Munda philosophy is akin to the philosophy of Spinoza. Munda philosophy is akin to 'pantheism' of Spinoza, who thought that the world is appearance of God who is immanent everywhere'.

When Singbonga was rising to Heaven as the Asur women clung to His clothes, He caught them by their hair-knots and threw them off. The one who fell on the hill became buru bonga (a hill spirit), the one who fell into river became *ikir bonga* (a spirit of river), the one who fell on high ground became *nager bonga* (spirit of high-ground), then the one who fell on high hill became *marang buru bonga*, the one who fell on the wooded spot became the *deasuli bonga*, the one who fell on pebble spot became *chandil bonga.*

As per the Munda tradition, when these bongas are not appeased with proper food and drinks, they with the permission of Singbonga, can cause illness in humans and animals. In order to appease these bongas, the Mundas have to offer sacrifice—food and drinks to them.

Thus, Mundas are often seen making offering of food (including hens and goats) and drinks in appeasement of these *bongas.* They however, do not worship them but only make offering for appeasement. These *bongas* also take care of the spots where they fell during the ascension of Singbonga to heaven, as well as reside in them. To a person unfamiliar with the Asur legend, it will appear that the Mundas worship hills, rivers, trees and nature.

The question here however arises when do the Mundas worship Singbonga—on what occasions? As per tradition, Singbonga has to be worshipped everyday in general and during festivals in particular. When Singbonga has to be worshipped, the worship has to be performed under a Shorea robusta (*sal/ sakhua* tree), because it is believed that Singbonga comes down from heaven when implored and rests particularly on a *sarjom daru* (*sakhua tree*). Therefore, every Munda household should have a sarjom tree in its courtyard. Sarhul—the festival of flower usually observed in spring, is the biggest festival of the Mundas during which Singbonga is worshipped in a grand way.

Mundas are monotheist in the sense that they worship only Singbonga, the Supreme Spirit. They are not polytheist as it commonly appears when they offer sacrifices to so many *bongas* (spirits). This is not worship but is just a performance of sacrifice (offering of food and drinks) in appeasement of a particular *bonga* (spirit) who may be in need of it.

With monotheism and pantheism as basic tenets, Munda philosophy could well be discussed in comparison to the Advaita philosophy of Shankara.

Man, God, Sex and Soul

The nature of a man is similar to the nature of the God he worships. In order to understand a person, one has to understand the kind of God the person believes in.

Man is the highest creature among animate and inanimate beings that Singbonga, the God of the Mundas, created. He created Man and Woman with intelligence, someone who can understand Singbonga more than others do, with whom Singbonga can relate.

Man is not the *Master* of Creation, like in the Bible—where the Creation is placed before the Man to rule over[7]. Since Man is endowed with intelligence, he has to be Singbonga like in nature and since Singbonga cares and provides for all, Man too should care and provide for all. In other words, Man has to play as the caretaker of all the beings in creation, not its destroyer. The moment he tries to destroy or create problems for the existence of any of the created beings, Singbonga will bring about destruction. Or destruction will naturally follow—just as it happened in the Asur Legend. Man has to play his role as Caretaker of Creation, and not as Master of Creation. Only Singbonga is the Master and none else.

If Man has to work only to fulfil his greed whole day and the whole night, this will only bring destruction.

Man has to work during the day and rest at night—soon after night falls. Songs and dances have been created for man in order to relax.

Man and Woman are created at the same time, from the same stuff, unlike in Christianity where the Woman is created out of the bones of Man, after the Man. In the *Sirjan Kani*, Singbonga made the idols of Man and Woman simultaneously, and not one after the other (Man and then the Woman). This is why gender equality is the norm in the social structure of Munda Tribes, coming down straight from the Legend of Creation.

The soul, on the other hand, is that which survives the body after the death of a person, and is called *'ji'* (*Hasda* Mundari dialect) or *'jiu'* (in *Naguri* Mundari). Though Mundas are unhesitating and staunch believers in the *soul* as distinct from the body and as surviving later, they distinguish between its various functions. They also use a term *'roa'*, which in itself is not *Ji* (soul). They use another term—*Umbul* (shade), which too, in itself is not *Ji* (soul). But collectively, the two: *Roa* and *Umbul*, form the *Ji* (soul), as one complete entity. But this is only when the person in whom *Roa* and *Umbul* both rest as Ji, is alive. When the person dies, *Roa* gets separated from *Umbul* and can either move to *sirma* (heaven) or take rebirth. The *Umbul* does not move to *sirma*, neither does it take rebirth. If the person dying lived a noble life, the *Umbul* is welcomed back into the house and given a corner to reside. The *Umbul* of the dead ancestor lives in the house itself and protects the members every minute.

The *ji* (soul) is considered the efficient cause of all the processes of the bodily life. It is therefore said to be present everywhere in the whole body, and to act. During a dream it is *roa*, not the *umbul* in the *ji*, which leaves the body and wanders about: it is not good to wake people abruptly without leaving the *roa* time to re-enter the body.

After the death of a person, when the *'umbul'* has been recalled to the house, it is called *'orah-bonga'* (house spirit). Mundas hold an elaborate function to recall the *umbul* of a person after his death.

Further, *Ji* (soul) is the principle of life found not only in men, but also in animals and plants. In plants, however, it has only the vegetative power, in animals moreover it has the faculty of sensuous perception and the appetitive and locomotive faculties; in man, in addition to all these, it has reason and rational appetitive or will. The ji as endowed with reason and will, has also *mon* (mind).

Presence of concepts like *ji*, *roa and umbul* in the concept of soul, *bitarpur* (inner dwelling place), *porom dishom* (the country beyond), *sirma* (sky or heaven) make the study of Munda concept of Man and Soul very exciting.

❑

CHAPTER 2

Man and Woman: Day and Night

Man became the Earth and Woman the Wind

The Almighty created the Earth with the help of Earthworm, Fish and the Crab; and when he saw his beautiful Creation, he felt happy. But the very next moment he became sad.

'Something is missing,' he said to himself, rubbing his forehead.

'What is missing?' his Inner-Self asked him.

'I do not know, but I feel that something more should be there in the Creation,' the Almighty replied.

The Inner-Self of the Almighty went into a deep thought. 'In order to discover something, one has to go quiet and just ponder and ponder over it,' the Inner-Self murmured to the Almighty. After a while, he opened his eyes and looked at the Almighty, smiling.

'Aha! So you've got it. Tell me quickly,' the Almighty was now eager to know what his Inner-Self had discovered.

'You have to create a being who would be equipped with intelligence far superior to that of the existing ones. You have to create the Man.'

'Good, good. Great idea. But how do I create Man?'

'Well, you have created the Earth, haven't you? Take some soil from the Earth and make an idol of the Man. Then ask the wind to flow into it. Man will come alive.'

The Almighty followed exactly what his Inner-Self told him to, and prepared an idol of Man.

'Now, ask the wind to flow into the idol,' the Inner-Self directed the Almighty. The Almighty acted accordingly.

The Man was made of Soil and when the Wind entered it, Man and Woman came into being. Soil was the Man and the Wind was the Woman—together they became Human, and thus they came into being in this creation. No one came earlier, neither the Man nor the Woman; both came together at the same time, as one.

'When one will separate from the other, both will die,' the Almighty warned the Man and the Woman—the Earth and the Wind.

'When Earth gets divorced from Man, neither the Earth nor the Man will live,' the Almighty further explained to the Man and the Woman. 'So, you as Man should never divorce Earth, for just as you divorce Wind—the Woman, you cease being alive, similarly when you divorce Earth, you will cease being'.

God was happy when he saw that Man and Woman were intelligent and had rationality. He showed to them the vast field and told them: 'I give this earth to you and all its greenery, the fruit-bearing trees, the animals and aquatic creatures to live by. Since you are the most intelligent of the creatures, I appoint you as their caretakers. But, beware! Do not be their masters, you must take care of them so that they care you too'.

After a while, the Almighty came to the Man and the Woman and took them to the vast field.

'Look there. This is the Vast Field. Out of it you have to prepare land on which you will grow vegetables and foodgrains for your living.'

The Man set out with spades to prepare agricultural lands out of the Vast Field. He dug and dug in the field and prepared a plot of land for farming. Then, he dug again, and prepared another plot. Then yet another.

The Almighty had not visited the Man for quite a while and thought He will see him and find out how he was doing. He saw the Man busy digging the field, with his tongue stuck out long, sweat all over the body.

'Grandson, when did you prepare this land?' the Almighty pointed to the first plot of land and asked.

'Today,' said the Man.
'And that one?'
'Today,' said the Man.
'And that one?
'Today,' said the Man.

The Almighty realised that the Man had been digging ever since he was asked to dig the field to prepare a piece of land for farming.

'If the Man goes on working like this, he will soon die,' the Inner-Self told the Almighty. 'Set a time for his rest. Make Day and Night'. The Almighty nodded. He asked the Sun to go down and hide itself.

When the Sun hid itself, the Man went back home to the Woman. As he was very tired, he soon fell asleep.

When the Man had regained his energy after a good rest, the Almighty directed the Sun to appear again.

Thus, the Almighty divided Time into Day and Night, so that when it is Day, Man would work and when Night came, Man would go back home and take rest with the Woman.

Thus, the Day and the Night came into being and ever since they have been coming and going. Man became the Earth and the Woman became the Wind. If Man divorces the Earth, he will die. If Woman divorces the Wind, she will cease to be.

–The Munda Myth of Creation

*

In commemoration of the creation story, the Mundas in Bombolkera village of Simdega district in Jharkhand, hold a week-long festival called *Khuntkati Mela* beginning from December 26 every year to revere and worship the Earth. During this week, everyone is to respect and love Mother Earth. No one is allowed to do anything that may pain the Earth, because from the Earth the Human is created, and to it the Human returns. Villagers are prohibited to spit, to plough, to cut trees and break stones and hills. On the first day of the week-long celebrations, the *pahan* (Munda priest) keeps fast and offers prayers to the Earth, followed by songs and dances in thankfulness to the Earth to mark the occasion. '*Earth is holy and so are the Humans,*'—their *durang* (song) goes[8].

*

Two important concepts: 'god' and 'man', are the key concepts that control a man or woman from birth till death (and even after death), his relationship with other human beings, his relationship with the environment he lives in, his attitude towards life and world, his attitude towards other animate or inanimate beings in the Creation. Understanding of these two concepts also influences a society, a group, a religion; a society's relation with other societies, a group's relation with other groups or a religion's relation with other religions.

Soon after a child takes birth, his mind being tabula *rasa*[9] but with innate potentials to develop concepts, inculcates the concept of 'god' and 'man'—first from his parents, then from his relatives and neighbours, and then from the society and the religion his parents adhere to and teach him. Unknowingly, a child starts growing up with a particular concept of god and man, and when he becomes an adult, he starts living his life getting controlled with these two concepts at every step of his life. With these concepts he completes his life on earth and either goes to hell (or heaven) or goes no where. Thus, the concepts of *god* and *man* are what substantially make his worldview, set of beliefs and practices. Every action of the man, his thoughts and deeds, every act of commission and omission is directed and controlled by his understanding of the concept of god and man, though he is unaware of the same. The two crucial global concerns that plague humanity today—communal discord and the environmental degradation are products of these concepts of god and man.

The philosophy of Munda tribes proclaims a completely different concept of man (and also Creation) in which man being superior in reason among beings in the creation, is assigned the task of taking care of the creation rather than being its 'master' as some philosophies, particularly the Christian philosophy propounds, and unconsciously followed by people with Vedic concept of *Aham Brahmashmi* (I am the Absolute), the theory that explains the unity of macrocosm and microcosm—wherein the Part reflects the Whole, and concept of rebirth—both of which when expanded further, envisage *soul* in every being. Consumerism is not possible in Vedic philosophy, but Christian philosophy has managed to attract the followers of Vedic tradition into rationalised consumerism.

The Yahweh of Abrahamic tradition, the polytheism in Vedas ultimately leading to monotheism—one Brahman in the *end of the Vedas* (Vedanta), Jainism and Buddhism's denial of a creator deity, the Singbonga in Tribalism (or Tribal Philosophy)—all of which are different words of the same name—has been a matter of serious quest for humanity for ages in order to understand life and find meaning in living.

Tribal Philosophy is yet to come into being in the written form like that of established philosophies of the world; but this philosophy can be extracted immensely and richly from the Tribes' folktales, folklores, myths and legends, social and religious practices and worldview. Myths like *Sirjan Kani* (story of Creation), *Asur Kani* (Asur Katha), traditions like *Buru Bonga* (Hill Spirit), *Ikir Bonga* (River Spirit), *Gram Deoti* (Village Goddess), *Daru Bonga* (Tree Spirit), *Soso Bonga* (*Bhelwa Pujan*), *Karam Bonga* (Karam Spirit) etc., various rituals performed from birth to death of a person in Tribalism (Tribal Religion)—all these offer ample philosophical tenets. Tribalism can be best understood when compared with other philosophies, for people view something from a standpoint. Comparison helps something stand out, and everyone is always comparing something or the other with his own standpoint all the time.

While a few tenets of Tribal philosophy bear similarity with some tenets of Vedic philosophy, most stand in stark contrast. On the other hand, Christianity that has its origin from equally older tradition—the Abrahamic tradition that includes Judaism and Islam too, Tribal philosophy may stand completely alien and aloof, particularly in things like consumerism, industrialisation, mining and environmental exploitation (*God said: Let us make man in our own image, in the likeness of ourselves, and let them be masters of the fish of the sea, the birds of heaven, the cattle and all the wild animals and all the creatures that creep along the ground. Genesis 1:14*). In Tribal Philosophy, *man* is the '*caretaker*' of the Creation, and not the 'master'. It is due to this '*caretaker*' concept that there still is community land-holding system in the Mundas—land is community property and not personal, and man inherits land property as a community from his forefathers only to till and yield food for his sustainance. He has to '*take care*' of the land, the forest, the trees, the herbs etc, and pass them onto his next generation just as he had received them *undamaged* from his forefathers. The philosophy of '*Eminent Domain of the State*' that the British followed stems from this Christian philosophy. The Tribal Philosophy, however, stands at complete opposite to this. Interestingly, independent India too, clings on to this philosophy, and adherents of Tribal Philosophy lose court cases while trying to save their lands to land acquisition bids of governments for mining and industries. Tribal Philosophy, if espoused well, can well become *the philosophy* of modern times to correct and align attitudes to environment, and to promote human existence at a time when human existence itself is at stake due to ecological and environmental issues.

–The Mundas

Born from the Earth

In the ancient days, the entire region was filled with forests. And in the forest, there lived a famous sage.

One day, the king of the country was in the forest on a hunting expedition with his army. When darkness fell, he started worrying about where he would spend the night.

'Wherever I spot fire and smoke, I should go there and spend the night', he thought.

He ran his eyes over the area and spotted a place in the distance from where smoke billowed out. The king moved towards it and found that it was the hut of a sage.

The Sage had a cow, which gave milk according to the wishes of the sage.

The Sage looked after the king with utmost care. He fed him with lots of milk and curd.

'Where do you get so much milk and curd from?' the king asked the Sage.

'I have a cow that gives as much milk as you ask of her,' the Sage replied.

When the king heard this, his greed intensified, and he asked the Sage to hand over to him the wonder cow.

'I only have this cow to feed me and nothing else. So, I am sorry, I cannot give you the cow,' the Sage pleaded with the king.

But the greedy king was in no mood to take "no" for an answer. He tied the cow with the help of a huge rope that the Sage used for drawing water from the well, and started to pull the cow away.

When the cow saw that the king was taking her away forcibly, without the consent of her master, she got angry.

She dashed the Earth with her horns, making a hole in it. And behold! Thousands of soldiers came out from the hole, armed with bows and arrows, axes and spears. They engaged the king and his army in a battle. Within minutes, the king's army perished, the king was slain on the spot and the cow was saved.

The Sage looked at the hole in the Earth. Soldiers were still emerging from it. He rushed up and blocked the hole with a stone. He turned towards the soldiers and told them—'This kingdom is yours now'.

The men started living in the forest, eating fruits and roots. They were known as Sing Mundas, because they had been born from the Earth with the help of the wonder cow's horns. Because the Sage had blocked the hole in the Earth with a stone, the Mundas continue to put a stone on the graveyard of their dead after a person is buried. This act is known as *sasangdiri*—stone on the grave[10].

–From the Store of Munda Folktales

*

What god(s) are to Vedic and Christian population, Nature is to the ethnic tribal communities in India, and so is the case even with the Mundas. Their myths and legends would necessarily have to have the element of Nature in them. Amidst the dense forest, immense natural resources, hills and dales, streams and rivers, rich flora and fauna, they lived in geographical locations with beauty and grace. In the history of man, facing strange problems and unfavourable situations, the Mundas, the first few groups to clear forests and take to settled agricultural life, formed their distinctive lifestyle and culture having fought through wild animals and equally wild Nature. Today scholarly presentations of research papers and findings are made at seminars and discussions on tribal culture, but at that time there was no such thing. Ancient man who had to fight against Nature and wild animals for his survival could not probably have paid attention to luxurious thing like 'culture' at that time. His day to day life was mostly spent on food gathering, safeguarding himself against Nature and wild animals, coexisting with them rather than fighting against them, creating his own world and worldview in a manner befitting to the geographical surrounding he lived in. He did not realise when this lifestyle of his actually had, without his knowledge, taken the form of a 'culture'. This 'culture' was naturally centred on and around Nature, passed into successive generations a life style of shared values.

The word "Munda" is a generic word, and even anthropologists agree on this. The Munda linguistic family of tribes includes tribes like the Munda (better known as 'Komapt Mundas' in the fraternity), Santhal (Santhal Mundas), Ho (Ho Mundas), Kharia (Kharia Mundas), Bhumij (Bhumij Mundas), Juang, Asur, Kherwar, Kora, Turi, Korwa, Agaria, Savara and Gadava. Several groups of the original Munda group had gone their separate ways in the days of the Munda migration from Ruidasgarh (Rohtashgarh) to Chotanagpur (according to S.C. Roy about 600 BC[11]) or even earlier[12]. The religions and the concepts of god and man in these groups seem to have much in common with that of the Mundas (Kompat Mundas)[13]. With the onslaught of modernism, many of their folktales and folklores and myths are dying fast, being forgotten even by the tribes themselves. The rich philosophical tenets that are hidden in these things also may die out if they are not documented now and brought into the mainstream of the written world.

Scholars like Dr. Ram Dayal Munda, a former professor of Indology at the Department of South Asian Studies, University of Minnesota, who later came back to Chotanagpur to serve his own people, have tried to bring out Munda understanding of god and man through folklores, folktales and legends in a few books like *Adi Dharam, Saled* et al. Dr. Rose Kerketta, a former professor of Ranchi University, in her book *Kharia Lok-kathayen* has made a similar attempt. Jagdish Trigunayat in his book *Munda Lok-kathayen* too has come out with the same kind of attempt by collecting folktales and legends in book form. But these books have not dwelt upon things philosophically. Myths like *Sirjan Kani* (Story of Creation), *Asur Kani* (Asur Katha), traditions like *Buru Bonga* (Hill Spirit), *Ikir Bonga* (River Spirit), *Gram Deoti* (Village Goddess), *Daru Bonga* (Tree Spirit), *Soso Bonga* (Bhelwa Pujan), *Karam Bonga* (Karam Spirit) etc, various rituals performed from birth to death of a person in Munda groups—all these offer ample scope to extract philosophical tenets for Tribal Philosophy.

It is now an established theory, both by anthropologists and historians, that the Mundas are one of most ancient races of the Indian sub-continent, and that the word 'Munda' finds mention in the Vedas ample number of times[14]. "At this point, closer inspection of the language of the Vedas extends a helpful hand. About 300 words that occur in the Rigveda are not Indo-Aryan or indo-European but come from elsewhere. Many come from Munda, a group of languages still spoken in parts of India".[15] Famous anthropologist S.C. Roy, quoting Hunter's *Annals of Rural Bengal*, says 'an unclaimed ignoble hordes who occupy the background of Indian History as the jungle once covered the land to prepare the soil for better forms of life'[16].

The word 'Munda' finds mention in the Mahabharata as well. (*Mundanetan Hanismami Danabaniba Basaba*: 'I shall kill the Mundas even as Indra killed the Danavas)[17]. The Mundas were believed to have sided with the Kauravas in the Mahabharat battle gainst the Pandavas[18], because Krishna, was supposed to have killed their king Jarasandha in a battle of supremacy. *'Mahabharat ke samay Magadh Brihadrathbanshi Samrat Jarasandh ke adhipatya me tha. Aang, Bang, Kaling, Pundra aur Chedi (Chhattisgarh) uske adhikar me the. Mahabharat me uska parakram ka bistrut varnan hae. Wah Shiv ka upashak that. Asur uski Jati thi.)..Mahabharat ke anusar Jarasandh ka ant Mahabharat yudh ke 14 varsh pehle Arthat 1220 kali sambat me hua tha.* (In the time of the Mahabharat, Magadh was ruled by King Jarasandh of the Brihadrath dynasty. Anga, Banga, Kalinga, Pundara and Chedi (Chhtisgarh) were parts of his empire. The *Mahabharat* describes in detail his tales of valour. He was a worshipper of Shiva. He belonged to the Asur fold. According to *Mahabharata*, Jarasandh died 14 years before the battle of Mahabharat in 1220 Arhat Kali Samvat).[19]

Asurs, an elder branch in the Munda tribes, had arrived in Chotanagpur region ahead of other Munda tribes during migration and still inhabit in Netarhat region of Jharkhand.

'The Asur, a Kolarian tribe of Chotanagpur and near kinsmen of the Mundas, especially name the Dhaulagir and the Mainagir as the localities in which they dwelt of old.'[20] While Munda also is a name of a leading tribe residing mostly in Central Indian states, it is a generic term for Austro-Asiatic tribes[21].

The Mundas have committed little to writing and till recent centuries, their tradition was mostly oral. Through folktales and folklores, they passed down their past, which often cannot be taken as history, except partly with corroboration with other references found in other traditions. The efforts of anthropologists cannot go beyond a certain stage and for some mysterious reason historians have long despised the ancient settlers' past to conjure up facts and put them together into what can be properly termed as the history of the Mundas. Not even a chapter of decent length is allotted to these people in any standard work on the history of India, including the ancient Indian scriptures and epics, except calling them names at sporadic places.

But to the solace of searching minds, many scholars agree on certain points. The Asurs were kinsmen of the Mundas and that the Indus Valley Civilisation belonged to them, and that they were engaged in battle with the Indo-Aryans on several occasions in the past[22]. The Mundari history, if history it can be called, "Hardly passes beyond the region of mythical legends. And even such myths that have been passed down to the Mundas by their ancestors hardly carry a searching mind beyond the period of Aryan occupation of the Indian subcontinent. The traditions of the Mundas speak of their residence in other parts of India before they finally entered Chotanagpur,"[23] where they now have been concentrated for the past several centuries. One tradition names *Seya Sandi Bir* as the original home of the Mundas but this place cannot be identified by scholars; and even the word can no longer be found in Mundari lexicon.

Another Munda Cosmogonic legend names Ajabgarh as the place which was first raised out of the Primeval Ocean and where the first parents of the Mundas are said to have been created by Singbonga. But this tradition, according to Roy, has been borrowed from the Hindus 'who appear to have been acquainted with the geological truth of the Age of Fishes as Matsya Purana suggests[24]. According to the Munda story of Creation, crab, fish and earthworm are supposed to have helped *Singbonga*, the Supreme God of the Mundas, to create the Earth. But interestingly, 'geologists tell us that animals allied to the crabs were in abundant in the Primary Epoch'[25], and even to this day during festivals like Sarhul, observed by the Mundas and other tribes, crabs are caught and offered in the puja to *Singbonga* because they lent support to Him in creating the Earth. Whatever be the case, that the ritualistic extant of this legend is still found verily in the Munda festivals is a fact.

There is also the Theory of Leumeria[26], now a submerged hypothetical continent, which is supposed to have once connected India with Madagascar and Africa, where the Mundas originated; but this legend seems fit only for fiction.

The tradition of the Mundas also talks of their residing beside a *Marang Buru* (Big Mountain), probably the Himalayas. Sir Alexander Cunningham says that the hill district between the Beas River in Punjab and the River Tons were in ancient times known as the Kuninda-Des, Kulinda-Des or Kulnda[27]. The name Kulinda, it seems probable enough, is the name applied for the Kolarian Tribes as the Mundas are also known.

Various folklores and legends of the Munda Tribes name North India as their ancient home, and it seems more probable than other legends that talk of places like Lemuria, because similar line of view is made even by Indo-Aryan tradition, which probably had been the rival of the Mundas at that time. In an Indo-Aryan tradition that relates "how Yayati, an ancestor of Jarasandha made a division of his empire among his five sons, and in the tenth generation from Turvasu, four brothers, Pandya, Kerala, Kola and Chola divided India among themselves"[28]. The Northern India, it is said, was allotted to Kola, whose descendants were known as Kolarian or as Kols too; these days often used in pejorative connotation by men who have little sense of history or simply spurn it.

In the Rig Veda, we hear of several powerful leaders of the Mundas, they being called 'Dasyu' because of the rivalry that existed between the two races. Thus, we hear of 'hundred ancient cities of Dasyu leader 'Sambara'[29] (*Sombaru* of our days, probably due to his birth on Monday) the hundred cities of Vangrira[30] and the ninety-nine cities of the Dasyu leader Pipru[31] all in Northern India. The cities of the Kolarian leaders mentioned here were probably settlements at the most, because they were still pastoral and so was the condition of the Indo-Aryans, who probably envied the Mundas. This settlement must have provided some space for development of serious things like culture and philosophy. The Indo-Aryans had better bards who kept the story of struggles alive, told usually from their point of view. Thus, most of culture, religion and philosophy that the Mundas have today, must have developed outside the initial settlements, probably in the Central Indian region after they migrated from Northern India to develop their own art, culture, literature, philosophy and religion. This must, however, have happened slowly, over the centuries, as there are records that the Mundas took part in Mahabharata battle. The partaking in the battle is an indication that Mundas as a people were a force to recon with and groups like the Kauravas and Pandavas which went to battle, solicited their partaking.

Hence baring Leumuria—which is mostly fiction, in places like Punjab and Ajabgarh—which scholars like S.C. Roy place somewhere in modern-day Uttar Pradesh, the Mundas must have resided there for long. Later Munda tradition, according to Roy himself, talks of their migration to Kalangjar, Garh Chitra, Garh Nagarwar, Garh Daharwar, Garh Pali, Garh Pipra, Mandar Pahar, Bijnagarh, Lakhnougarh, Nandangarh, Rijgarh and Ruidasgarh and then to Chotanagpur of Jharkhand through Omedanda[32]. Present day Mundas, however, vividly recall their staying at Ruidasgarh—modern-day Rohtash, and arriving in Chotanagpur through Omedanda in Budmu of Ranchi.

As stated before, the Munda family of tribes consist mainly of the Mundas, the Santals, the Hos, the Kharia (or Kheria) and the Bhumij, Juang and other Mon-Khmers.

These tribes have striking linguistic as well as cultural similarity, and it is difficult to say at which point of time they branched out into different groups.

Both Munda and Santal tradition speak of an ancestor Risha Munda, who denied the hand of his daughter to the son of a Kharwar ruler, following which the Kharwars attacked Risha Munda at night. This happened in Rohtashgarh. The surprise attack made the Mundas leave Rohtashgarh and migrate to the present day Chotanagpur, entering through Omedanda, some 50 kilometres to the west of Ranchi. It is after this point that a group, later to be known as the Santals, parted ways with their original kin[33], who still hold the name 'Munda'. Santals travelled alongside the River Damodar and settled in Shikharbhum—present day Hazaribagh, and spanned across the place over time. Later, similar divisions further must have happened in the original group, generating sub groups like Hos, Kherias, Bhumij etc.

According to Encyclopaedia Mundarica of J.B. Hoffman, one group of the Mundas could not pronounce 'd' in the word *'Hod'*, which stands for *'man'* in Mundari and hence on repeatedly being reminded of its demerit, decided to separate from the main group and continued to pronounce *'Ho'* for 'man' and later came to be called *'Ho'*[34]. This group that originated from the Munda family, came to be known later as simply *'Ho'* and is called so even today. The group presently resides in Kolhan region of Jharkhand state [the word 'Kol' can be noticed here too]. Interestingly, Chaibasa region is found to have been inhabited during pre-historic age and sharp stone implements have been recovered from this region by archaeologists[35]. The men are called "Ho: a member of the Ho branch of the Munda race.... Mundas and the Hos stand in same relation as the Dutch and the Flemings, same race, same language, but political and geographical separation. When the Census report speaks of the *Ho* language, it is a misnomer. There is no *Ho* language. The *Hos* speak Mundari. Their dialect is scarcely different from the Hasada [one of two forms of Mundari, the other being Naguri] dialect, except that when in the latter a cerebral 'd' stands in between two vowels, it is generally dropped in the Ho dialect... The Mundas, as a rule do not call themselves Mundas; this name has been given to them by other people. They call themselves 'Hodo-ko' –'the Men', and likewise the Hos call themselves 'Hoko', which is contraction of 'Hodo-ko'. The other Mundas often call themselves 'Ho Mundako', owing to their dialectical peculiarity."[36]

Likewise, separation for different reasons by different groups at different point of time resulted in groups like Santal, Kheria, Bhumij and others. According to a Kheria tradition, which Colonel E.T. Dalton too talks about, a Munda chieftain had two young sons and he wanted to choose one of them to inherit his status. He got a horse and asked the two to mount on it in turn. One who displayed the superior skill was to be chosen. The horse was tall it was difficult for the young boys to mount on it as they were yet to have the training. The elder boy was given the first chance. But as soon as he saw the horse, he went in search of a ladder to mount on to it. The second boy, who was watching his elder brother, then ran towards the horse and mounted on it in a single attempt. The father chose the second son to inherit his status and the first boy was assigned to take care of the land. The descendants of the first son were known as the Kheria, who became agriculturists as well as doubled as the *Kalo* (priest), while the second son inherited the position of Munda (chieftain)[37].

According to scholars, Mundas entered Chotanagpur in about 600 B.C. 'On different evidences, it is inferred that the Mundas entered Chotanagpur from the west in about 600 B.C.'[38] Unlike today, the region had been covered by very dense forest. Slowly, they spread out far and wide, and in later days came to reside under different provinces in Central India. In any case, the west part of Ranchi from where the Mundas are thought to have entered Chotanagpur is still covered by dense forest even today. Omedanda, a hilly region in the west of Ranchi which the scholars fix as the entry point, is still a dense forest. The entry of the Mundas must have taken place in small groups, and this continued for several decades and slowly, the settlement spread to different regions. Munda tradition talks of one Sutia Munda, a chieftain, who set up Sutiambe, a place on the east of present day Ranchi, as his seat of power. Sutiambe was located on a hill, and is still known by that name, located about 10 miles away from Ranchi near Pithoria, another famous place which, according to Dr. B.P. Kesri—who had his ancestral home in this village and where he lived his entire life—was an intersection point for traders who travelled different parts of the country for trade. Pithoria had shot to fame during Maurya and Gupta era as a point of traders' intersection, but it obviously was not the case during the days of Sutia Munda. After Sutia Munda, Munda tradition talks of another chieftain Madra Munda, to have chosen his adopted son instead of his natural son, as the ruler of his kingdom. This son was Phani Mukut Rai, who became the founder of Nagabanshi dynasty in the region. According to Ranchi Gazetteer (1917), the coronation of Phani Mukut Rai took place sometime after the *Hos* proceeded towards Kolhan region. Munda tradition puts the coronation in the First century AD, while Dr Kesri puts the time at 64 AD. Some traditions even say that some group of Munda men did not accept the decision of Madra Munda to hand over the reigns to the adopted son and hence they parted ways, creating smaller groups. It is during their stay in Chotanagpur and in its vicinity that there developed culture, folklores, folktales, tradition, worldview, religion and philosophy of the Munda family of tribes.

In course of time, the Oraons, belonging to the Dravidian linguistic group, entered Chotanagpur Plateau after losing their fort Ruidasgarh to their enemies in a battle, and the Mundas accepted them into their settlement and even settled them with lands. This historical incident took place in Mudma, about 30 kilometres west of Ranchi and even today the Oraons gather at Mudma to commemorate the incident during Mudma Mela, celebrated in the month of Aswin every year. As per the traditions, the Mundas after giving their lands in the west of Ranchi to the Oraons, moved south and prepared the land afresh by clearing forests there. This place came to be known as Khunti. But the Mundas while leaving their lands to the Oraons, appointed a man from their own fold as the *'Munda'* (headman) in each village of the region, who was to carry out day-today administrative affairs of the region. This arrangement is still prevalent and the headman of the Oraon villages in Ranchi and other areas is still a Munda by tribe. Much of the Munda culture, religion and philosophy developed in association with the Oraons, the two groups growing side by side.

Do the Munda Tribes Have a Philosophy?

It is impossible for a man to live without a philosophy. The choice, as Aldous Huxley puts it, is not 'between metaphysics and no metaphysics; it is always between a good metaphysics and a bad metaphysics'.[39] Just like a man, no human group can live without a philosophy. The worldview, the meaning of life and living, the meaning of living together, the ways, joys and sorrows of life—all these collectively sum up into what is known as the philosophy of a man or a group of humans. Things like God and Man, Soul and Knowledge, this world and world after death, outlook towards actions etc. form important aspects of philosophy of a man or group.

Unlike established traditions such as Hinduism, Christianity, Islam, Buddhism—which today have their philosophies in written form and hence established, the Munda tribes fall short of this, and in that sense, they lack a written body of philosophy, though they are one of the oldest races of humankind with developed culture and tradition. But, even the Hindu philosophy, which is one of the oldest in human civilisation, had an oral tradition and its philosophy that is imbedded in the Vedas and the Upanishads. It was in oral form, then a properly assigned group of men kept it vividly alive by knowing it by-heart and passing it from one generation to another through oral tradition till it was written down just a few centuries ago.

The Mundas being one of the oldest races in the world, have a rich body of folktales, folklores, tradition, culture, religious beliefs and practice, social beliefs and practice—all of which contain rich philosophy in them. These folktales, folklores, legends, tradition, culture, religious beliefs and practices, social beliefs and practices have developed by living together for several millennia as one family and living with other human groups side by side, sometimes as friends and sometimes as foes. The Munda group has lived with nature and has wondered about its energy, beauty, vastness and variety. One finds honest wonder and appreciation of the Munda tribes for nature in their folklores and folktales. From dealing with victories and losses in battles, journey through difficult terrains in search of a better and peaceful place to live in, often to an unknown destination, their legends dwell on things like how the different clans got their totems, how they celebrated joys and sorrows together as a people. The religion of the Mundas, as one finds it, is centred on nature, and Singboga is their Supreme Deity[40]. The legend of Creation—the *Sirjan Kani*, the legend of Destruction—the *Asur Kani*, the Legend of Procreation, traditions of *Buru Bonga* (Hill Spirit), *Ikir Bonga* (River Spirit), *Gram Deoti* (Village Goddess), *Daru Bonga* (Tree Spirit), *Soso Bonga* (*Bhelwa Pujan*), *Karam Bonga* (*Karam* Spirit) etc. and various rituals performed from birth to death of a person in Tribalism (Tribal Religion)—all these are rich and still prevalent among the Munda tribes.

A body of Munda philosophy has to be extracted from these folklores, folktales, legends, religious and social practices in order to build a systematic and written philosophy of the group, which would be as rich as those of the other established philosophical traditions of the world.

Since the beginning of human civilisation, the human mind has always wondered about creation, linking its outcome to a Creator that different philosophical traditions call 'God'. The 'Unmoved Mover' of Aristotle, the 'Yahweh' of Abrahamic tradition, the Eternity of Creation according to Vedic thinkers, who later attribute natural phenomena to gods—the line of thought that in later days culminates in *Advaitism* of Sankaracharya and Singbonga in the philosophy of Munda Tribes—all point to a quest for a Supernatural Being who may well have been the Origin, the *Alpha* and the *Omega*.

❑

CHAPTER 3

Singbonga: The Tribal God

The Munda Family of Tribes, as stated earlier is a conglomeration of many tribes, at least 20, the chief among them include the Mundas, Santals, Hos, Kherias, Bhumij, Birhor, Koda, Turi, Asur, Korwa, Juang, Savara, Gadaba among others. S.C. Roy writes, "Points of vocabulary, in details of grammatical forms, and in principle of language building, appear to establish a close connection between Kolarian Mundari, Santali, Bhumij, Ho, Birhor, Koda, Turi, Asuri, Korwa, Kurku, Kheria, Juang, Savara and Gadaba dialects of India, on the one hand, and, on the other, the Sakei and Semang dialects of Malay Peninsula, the Assamese, Bersis, and Mon-Khmer languages including Khasi dialects, the dialects of the aborigines of Malacca Isles, the Dippil, Turbul, Kamilaroy, Wodiwodi, Kingki, Wailwun, Toungguroung and other dialects of Australian tribes…."[41]

There is however, a tribe that still retains the original name Munda tribe, and hence it is the main representative tribe of the Munda group of tribes. It also happens to be the most orthodox in terms of language and culture, having withstood onslaughts of socio-political and other changes in recent days. The concept of God of this tribe, thus, can be safely accepted as the most orthodox and original. Though other tribal groups such as Santal, Ho and Kheria too have nearly the same kind of notion of God, they may differ slightly in their understanding of the subject. Over the years, groups like Santals and Kherias have been influenced by the Indo-Aryan civilisation, but not the Munda and the Ho tribes.

It is usually observed that the Mundas worship Nature. The common world knows the Mundas as Nature worshippers, worshipping trees, rivers, land, hills etc. Festivals like *Sarhul* and *Baba*, *Karam* etc, wherein a Nature is worshipped, establish the Nature worship tradition of the Mundas. This, however, is a misrepresentation of fact and there is more to it than meets the eye.

Singbonga is the Supreme God of the Munda tribe, who resides in *sirima* (Heaven). This Supreme God of the Mundas is All-good, Omniscient and Omnipotent, Maker, Master and Preserver of all things animate and inanimate.

In order to understand Singbonga, the Supreme God, it is necessary here to narrate the Munda legend of the Asur: '*The Asur Kani*'. This is a legend that is narrated often at festivals, gatherings and such other public functions, and obviously the narration differs, mostly due to the personal lack of expertise on the part of the individual narrators.

The Asur Kani

"That one who is in heaven we call Singbonga. Both husband and wife (Singbonga and his wife) are conversing with each other. Theirs was the first marriage, the first love. Singbonga is seated on a golden throne; he holds a golden sceptre.

At the time they were conversing with each other saying: 'The Asurs have little rice, and each but one bullock. The heifer with long straight horns, the cow with turned down horns, both complain to Singbonga: *the lotus covered tank, the ponds full of marsh flowers are drying up. We too find no food. Tree and shrub, grass and herb, all are withering. The creeping insects and the flying insects and the birds do no longer find water; they do not find food.'*

In heaven Singbonga was reached and was scorched by the heat (emanating from the Asurs furnaces). Seated on the golden throne he heard (these plaints) and he got angry. He took up his old sword and his worn shield, saying: 'I am going to cut these Asurs to pieces.' Then his wife said to him: 'Don't! Alone thou will not overcome them. They are numerous. They work their bellows by night and by day. Thou on the contrary art alone, in a fight with sword and bow, thou canst not overcome them. Outwit them by wisdom and craft,' she told him. 'Yes, alright,' he said.

Then he sent the fearless king crow and the watchful shrike as messenger to the Asurs. These two said: 'Listen! We have brought you a message, we have come with a request. If you blow the bellows by night, then do not blow them by day; and if you blow them by day, do not blow them by night. The tanks with its floating lotuses, the banks with their marsh flowers, are drying up, the heifers with long straight horns, the cow with crooked horns, do no longer find water, they do no longer find food', saying this the two birds said. 'The creeping insects and the flying insects and birds do no longer find water and food. On earth the grasses and herbs, the trees and shrubs are withering. In heaven Singbonga feels the heat and gets scorched,' they said.

Those Asur said: 'We ourselves are Singbonga, we ourselves are the great deity (i.e., we are the masters). We obey no orders. We had our own dawn and sunset before Singbonga, the Sun God, had his (i.e., we existed before him). Nobody is greater than we are. We will blow the bellows by night and will blow them by day,' saying this they replied. 'We hold together like plantains in a bunch, like mangoes spitted in the petioles of a twig, (i.e., we are numerous and united). We secure our daily food and more by repairing broken ploughshares (i.e., we are rich and depend on nobody). We obey no orders'.

They strew charcoal dust on the king-crow and iron dust on the shrike. 'Off! Be gone! To whom will you complain!'

They both went away. They complained to the Singbonga. 'Alas Sir, he and I have become outcaste'. 'Go back to your own caste. You will all look alike i.e., all king crows will henceforth look black and all shrikes grey,' he said to them. Then both went away and saw those of their own kind all alike.

Then he sent the golden vulture and the silver vulture. These two told the Asurs: 'Listen! We have brought you a message, we have come with a request'. The Asurs replied as they had done to the king crow and the shrike.

Then they struck both of them with hammer and with large pincers. 'Off! Be gone! To whom will you complain now?' they said.

Then Singbonga sent the worshipping lark and the observant crow to the Asurs. The Asurs threw charcoal dust on the crow and the ore dust on the lark.

Then Singbonga outwitted them by wisdom and craft. A servant was clearing and hoeing the eighty-one uplands, and the eighty-three rice fields. Then Singbonga sowed itch on that one's body. Then that one got itch-sores. When the sores had developed, Singbonga flew a golden hawk towards him, (i.e., went hunting with a golden hawk which he made to fly towards the servant). Then he told him: 'Come now! Let me try once with hoe.' Then that itch-covered youth replied: 'Owing to my itch-sores, I have covered the whole hoe with matter, I am not going to hand it to thee who art such a clean man'. Then Singbonga took him with the topknot of his hair and shook him. He fell out of his skin. With this skin Singbonga clothed himself and then went towards the Asurs. He swayed a leafed Vitex Negundo branch to drive away the flies.

Then he reached a village of the Asurs: 'I say! Will any of you engage a servant? I shall earn my wage by driving of the fowls (from the grain).' Then the Asurs said: 'Hey! You women have a look at him'. Then these looked at him, and having done so they say: 'Away', they say 'Be gone'. They spit. 'We won't, we don't engage such a servant. Our children would get infected. Go away, go to the hamlet yonder; there are two Mundas, an old man nicknamed Lutkum Hadam (with high cheek-bones) and an old woman Lutkum also thus nicknamed. They may engage thee; there have no children, they are childless. As for us, we won't'.

Then he went to those two.

'I say! My dear grandmother and grandfather are you at home? These two engage him as servant. Then he earns his wage by driving off the fowl (from the grain spread out to dry)'. Then one day he told them: 'Do get some eggs for me. I crave for them owing to my sores'. Then they got them for him. Then he went to the Asurs. He went to play with them. They had iron marbles, the itch-covered boy had eggs for marbles. Then the Asurs said to each other: 'Let us break his eggs and boil them'. 'Come on', they told him, 'put down the marbles'. He put them down. Then they could not hit his marbles. Then he said: 'Come, now you put down your marbles'. Then he rolled his marbles and he hit and broke the iron marbles. Then they were angry, because they had lost the game. 'Just wait a while, we shall denounce thee to old Lutkum and his wife. They had spread paddy on a mat for thee to watch it, and the fowl have eaten it all up,' they said.

They then reported to the old couple. The woman got angry: 'What are we going to eat? The fowl have eaten up everything. I told thee: *let us not engage this itch-covered boy as a servant*. Thou said, *we shall certainly engage him*. The itch-covered boy found his way back and picked up one of the grains of the paddy. He placed it on the mat, the mat was covered with it. He took it (the grain) to the house. He put it into the husking hole; the husking hole got filled. He put it in a basket; the basket got filled. He put it on a winnowing shovel; the shovel got filled. Then the old couple saw it. They asked him: 'Whose paddy hast thou stolen?'—'I have stolen no one's paddy, O grandmother and grandfather. It is ours that increases. Singbonga gives it to us'.

Then again on another day he asked them: O grandmother and grandfather. Make me some husk cakes. I crave for them owing to my sores'. Then they baked him some. Then taking them up he went to the Asur boys to play. Then they tell him: come on, play at half discs with thy husk cakes; put them down on the end'. Then they threw their half disc but did not hit. 'Come, now you put down your half discs,' he told them. Then he threw his. Theirs break: iron half discs are broken by half discs made of husk cake. Then they got angry because they had lost the game.

The he caused the Asur to run short of supply of iron. Then they said to the itch-covered youth: Come now! Do please examine (in divination) the rice grains for us'. He replied: 'I cannot even sit down, my sores are hurting, how can I divine for you?' Then they were starting back. He told them: 'Well, all right; I shall examine them lying down. Then you come back in the morning and I shall tell you the result'. Then the next morning they came back and asked: 'Well, what hast thou found?'—'Sacrifice a white cock in honour of Singbonga and you will find iron'. They sacrificed one, and rejoiced.

Then again, another day their iron ran short. Then once more they brought him rice grain. *(Divination examination in the Munda tribes is done with rice grains on a winnowing shovel).*

Sacrifice a white he-goat and you will find iron.'

Then they sacrificed a he-goat and found iron and rejoiced. Then they ran short of iron again and he examined the rice grain for them again, on the following day. 'Well, hast thou found it out for us?' they asked him. 'I have found it out for you. A human sacrifice has become necessary for you'. Then they were dumb-found. 'Alas! O itch-covered boy, where shall we find one (a human victim)?' they reply. —'Go to the Doisa country, to the Kukra country, there are Mundas there. Ask them, ask them whether they will sell some?'—'Alas, for what price they will sell us one? With what shall we buy him?' they say. Then he said: 'I give you this lump of gold as large as a pumpkin; go now and buy'. Then they went to the Doisa country and asked the people: 'I say! Do you sell men; if so we shall sacrifice (the one you sell us)'. 'Who wants to sacrifice our children? The ruffian! Thrash him! We have reared them from when they were little babies. What sacrifice wants (to sacrifice them). Thrash him'. Then they fled.

And they said to the itch-covered youth: 'Alas! We have not got any man'. –'How did you ask?'—'We said: I say, do you sell any child? If so we shall sacrifice it'. —'And then what happened?' 'We fled'. 'Here am I myself then, sacrifice me,' he said. I ail very much with these sores and a serious pus flows from them day and night

Then the old Lutkum Burha said: 'We shall not give thee up. Who will watch our household for us? To these two he says: 'Let them sacrifice me O grandmother and grandfather dear'. –'Who then will support us?'—'Before going away, I tell you this: you will surely be supported, do not worry. Let what I saw now remain (for ever unchanged) amongst the Mundas. Before going away I shall establish a public sacrifice under a tree in each village, he will sacrifice you to both of you once at flower feast, once at the *batauli* feast and once at the *mage* feast'. Then both replied: 'Alright then! We shall not forget this promise'.

Then the Asurs led him away in order to sacrifice him. Then before they sacrificed him, he said: 'Flay a white he-goat (to make bellows with the skin), make new bellow sticks, make a new nozzle (to the bellows), pound rice to flour, pound Eleusin millet to powder; let two maidens do the pounding before breaking their fast. Come, now plaster up (the furnace)'. Then just before entering the furnace, he told them: 'Let two maidens fast and work the bellows for three days. Let them work them day and night. Let them, on head cushions made of cotton thread, bring water in new earthen pitchers and let them extinguish the fire by sprinkling (water on) it with twigs of a mango tree. Come I am inside now, plaster me up'.

Then the two maidens worked the bellows day and night. Then, when three days had passed, they brought water in new pitchers on head cushions made of cotton thread; they extinguished the fire by sprinkling (water on) it with twigs of the mango tree. Then they battered and broke open the furnace with husking poles. Then he came out like the dawn, like the rising sun. He is covered with gold and silver ornaments; he holds in his hands a bowl and a plate. 'Is there much (much more treasure?)', they ask him—'Yes! Yes! There is much', he says. 'You are numerous, you will bring out a lot'. And then: 'You, men, all to the last, enter into the pit of the furnace', he says 'and bring all boys, otherwise later on you will rob from each other'. Then in the sky golden vulture and silver vulture are soaring. He tells these birds: 'Look at the feathers under your necks and at the main feathers of yours wings so as to find out (by divination) where the Asurs and their sons are, lest they hide themselves'. But the Asurs tell him: 'We are all here and have brought all our sons'.

Then, when all of them had entered: 'Fall to work, women, plaster up (the openings) with ore dust and charcoal dust'. They plastered them up. 'Go on, women, light the fire and blow the bellows, then pour charcoal on top of the furnace, and blow the bellows with energy. (Those inside) scream awestruck. 'Alas! Thou hast tricked us'.

'Steady, women, blow the bellows. They are quarrelling over the loot; they donot all get enough. Blow the bellows fast and quick'. Then blood flows out abundantly through the salg passage and through the hole where the nozzle is inserted. 'Alas! Thou hast tricked us, this is blood!' They tell him—'No, women (it is not). They are chewing betel leaf and betel nut, and spiting the (red) juice. Go to, women, blow the bellows fast and quick'. Then, when he judged that they were charred, he said: 'Batter and break down the furnace with your husking poles'.

Then they broke it with their husking poles. They found only bones, rattling dry bones. 'Alas! Thou hast tricked us', they said. 'We did not think that thou would act in this manner. Thou hast made us burn our men to death'—'What then?' he answered. 'I sent you the watchful shrike and the energetic king crow as messengers. You did not obey their order'. And then he asks them: 'Will you now obey my message and command?'—they say. 'Unless we obey, how can we possibly find our sustenance?—'All right then! I shall show you a way whereby you will be supported' he answered. Before going away I establish a witch-finder with a disciple. These two will endeavour to find you out in divination by means of broken rice, by means of the flame of a lamp or of a lighted flayed stem of the *Hibiscus cannabinus* or *Crotalaria juncea* plants. I tell you (order you) not to hide yourselves from the witch-finder and his aid. In the middle of each village there will be a Munda public sacrificer who will offer you sacrifices under a tree.

"After that he rises to heaven. And then those Asur women cling to his cloth. Then, he catching them by the topknots of their hair, threw them off. The one who fell on a hill became a buru bonga (a hill spirit); the one who fell into deep water became the ikir bonga (a spirit of the deep); the one who fell on high ground and near the head of a ravine became nage bonga; then the one who fell on a high became a karang buru bonga; the one who fell on a wooden spot became deasuli bonga, the one who fell ona wooden spot near a spring became chondor ikir bonga; the one who fell on a pebble or round stone became chandi bonga."[42]

—Encyclopaedia Mundarica

Singbonga: The Creator, Preserver and Destroyer

The Munda Legend of Creation—Srijan Kani talks of how the Supreme Spirit, Singbonga, who was Self-Created, created the world. He of course had his wife since the beginning of time, and the legend too mentions of her. The oral history of Munda Srijan Kani has already been narrated in the previous chapter.

Ironically, the co-creators of the earth—the Earthworm, Crab and the Fish, are in danger now, all by man's practice. Pesticides and chemical fertilisers threaten to wipe them away from the earth. Interestingly, just as their companion and creator the Almighty had said, if they die the earth may not survive long.

Singbonga is a Creator God. But He is the Creator only in a limited sense—in that he creates the World, trees, herbs, animals and plants there on, and not the water and aquatic creatures. He did not create 'Earth'—a primordial element, but found it out with the help of aquatic creatures. Singbonga is also the Preserver God. In the Asur Legend, He listens to the complaints of the earth creatures, and trees and herbs, who were withering due to the excessive heat created by the iron-smelting of the Asurs. Singbonga is the Destroyer God. Thus, comparing it with Hindu God (Generation, Operation and Destruction) of Brahma, Vishnu and Maheshwar, Singbonga singly plays all the roles. In other words, Singbonga is Brahma, Vishnu and Maheshwara in One.

Singbonga, however, does not seem much identical to the concept of Trinity: Father, Son and the Holy Spirit of Christianity, who are different in Persons, but at the same time One—as per the Christian idea of Unity of Godheads. Though in Christianity too, there is the idea of Creator (God the Father or Yahweh of Judaism), Destroyer (God the Father or Yahweh of Judaism), Preserver (Holy Spirit) and Redeemer (Christ, the Son), the Munda religious tradition, the same Singbonga, plays all these roles.

But unlike the Hindu tradition of incarnation of Gods in order to either Preserve—like in case of Vishnu Avatara, Singbonga does not seem to take incarnation too often. He adopts 'human form' twice to do something quickly and returns to his abode soon, as it happens with Asur Legend. Another time Singbonga took human form is when He indirectly taught the first couple how to have sex, narrated by the Mundas and other Munda Tribes alike in the Legend of Procreation.

Singbonga is complete Spirit with a power to adopt any form at will. Thus, though he is all Spirit, he can have forms too, if he so wishes. Therefore, Singbonga has Extension too, which he can make appear or disappear, with his power.

The Five Elements

From the Legend of Creation (*Srijan Kani*), it is inferred that the Primordial Elements were already present or rather they were existent, just as Singbonga existed, since the beginning of time. Water, air, ether, fire and earth were present. Along with them were present the 'aquatic life'—as Singbonga would go to them one after another –beginning with the fish, then to the crab, then to the tortoise and then finally to the earthworm—and ask each of them whether it could *make* the Earth. Or can it be said that the Earth was there submerged by the waters? And all that Singbonga is asking of the aquatic creatures is: can you find the Earth? Thus, it can also be said that 'earth' as a primordial element, too existed since the beginning of time just as water, air and ether. Singbonga is not the creator of these Primordial elements, but these are self-existent. So, Singbonga, unlike *Abrahamic* God (God in Judaism, God in Christianity and God in Islam) does not create out of nothing; but He 'makes' out of something. And what He does make: He makes the World, He makes the animals, the birds, trees, plants and herbs and finally the man and the woman with intelligence. He makes the man and the woman with intelligence something like Himself, so that they can offer him prayers and offerings. 'Something must come out of something' and this rule applies with Singbonga's creation.

As for the aquatic beings, if one goes by the Legend of Creation, they have not been created and are existent (or self-existent) since the beginning. But as these beings have a beginning and end—i.e., they are born in time and die in time (limited by Time) and perishable, the Legend of Creation does not explain how they could have been, since the beginning. Unlike the aquatic creatures, other Primordial Elements—water, air, ether and earth, are non-perishable. Thus, there is hardly any problem in their being accepted as existing since the beginning of time.

If Singbonga is the Creator of all things and he created with the help of the Primordial Elements, then even the aquatic beings had to be created by Him. Thus, Singbonga, unlike Yahweh of Abrahamic tradition is a Limited Creator. In Hindu tradition too, the Primordial Elements are self-existent, and the Creation comes out of them.

The *Sirjan Kani* (Legend of Creation) however, does not talk about Fire, the other Primordial Element found in Hindu tradition. But, in the Asur Legend, the Asurs are said to have discovered fire (Agneyasur),[43] and used fire while smelting iron. Thus, Fire must be discovered, just as Earth was discovered. The myth narrated by the Asurs (*Agarias*, as they too are called), Fire was discovered by the Asurs, a kinsman of the Mundas, who form part of the Munda Family of Tribes[44]. Thus, the five Primordial Elements—

Water, Air, Fire, Ether and Earth—were existent since the beginning of time. It is from these five elements that Singbonga creates (makes) things he created (made).

Singbonga: Personal or Impersonal

Singbonga generally appears to be an Impersonal God, who is in the form of Spirit. But at times like in the Legend of Creation, Legend of Asurs and Legend of Procreation, Singbonga appears to take human form with attributes and appear to the humans. Here He is a Personal God. But he keeps His Form only for a short duration and vanishes into his Spirit soon enough. And Mundas do not ever worship this Personal God, either by making his idols or just as He appeared. They worship Him in his Impersonal form.

Singbonga, thus, for most part, is a formless God, a Spirit, with the power to take physical form (become personal) if the need arises. He is with personal attributes. The Mundas however worship Him in his Impersonal form—i.e., residing in the heaven (*sirma re*), keeping a vigil upon his creation, the humans. He makes reward or award from his abode, the Heaven (*Sirma*) through the bongas (the spirit of the Asur women)—in that he allows them to do good or bad for the humans. Thus, after death of humans, Singbonga seems to have no control whatsoever over them or their souls.

Bonga

At first sight, it seems that Munda concept of God is Animism and Polytheism. Neither of it is however correct. The Munda tribe are not just Nature Worshippers. They worship only the Singbonga, the Supreme Sprit, residing in *Sirma*—Heaven.

But, Mundas are often seen worshipping at hills (buru), rivers (ikir), trees (daru) etc, on different occasions. The Asur Legend seems to give ample explanation to this religious act of the Mundas. The Asur Legend is the orally narrated tradition document (now brought in writing) on which the present system of religious feasts and rites observed by the Mundas is based.

In the Asur Legend, when Singbonga had destroyed the incessantly iron-smelting Asurs and was going back to His abode in Heaven, the Asur women clung on to different parts of His body. They told Him: 'We did not think that Thou wouldst act in this manner. Thou hast made us burn our men to death.'—'What then?', He answered. 'I sent you the watchful shrike and the energetic king-crow as messengers. You did not obey their orders.' This probably is the root incident why for the Mundas, messages come through birds and animals—usually called *omen*, and reading the omen and acting accordingly is important. And then He asked them: 'Will you obey my messages and commands?' 'Unless we obey, how can we possibly find our sustenance?'—'All right then, I shall show you a way whereby you will be supported,' He answered. 'Before going away I will establish a witch-finder with a disciple. These two will endeavour to find out in divination by means of broken rice, by means of the flame of a lamp or of a lighted flayed stem of the *Hibiscus cannabinus* or *Crotalaria junecia* plants. I order you not to hide yourselves from the witch-finder and his aide. In the middle of each village there will be a Munda public sacrificer who will offer you sacrifice under a tree.'

The sacrifice, thus, in the Singbonga tradition, has to be made under a tree. This, to bare eye, appears that the Mundas are worshipping the tree. As per belief, Singbonga loves to come and rest on a *Shorea robusta* (Sal tree) whenever He is invoked by the Munda priest (Pahan), and the Pahan has been instructed by Singbonga to worship and offer sacrifice at a tree, usually *Shorea robusta.*

When Singbonga was rising to Heaven as the Asur women clung to His clothes, He caught them by their hair-knots and threw them off. The one who fell on the hill became *buru bonga* (a hill spirit), the one who fell into river, became *ikir bonga* (a spirit of river), the one who fell on high ground and so on. The one who fell on pebble spot became *chandil bonga*. Chandil, a place near Steel City Jamshedpur in Jharkhand, must have been a residing place of the *chandil bonga.*

As per the Munda tradition, when these bongas are not appeased with proper food and drink, they, with the permission of Singbonga, can cause illness in the humans and animals. In order to appease these bongas, the Mundas have to offer sacrifice—food and drinks, to them. Thus, Mundas are often seen making offering of food (including hens and goats) and drinks (rice beer and country liquor) in appeasement of these bongas. They however, do not worship them, only make offering for appeasement. These bongas also take care of the spots where they fell during the ascension of Singbonga to heaven, as well as reside in them.

By mistake and lack of knowledge of the Asur Legend of the Mundas, the common eye thus assumes that the Mundas are worshipping hills, rivers, trees and so on.

The question here however arises: When do the Mundas worship Singbonga—on what occasions? As per tradition, Singbonga has to be worshipped everyday in general and during festivals in particular. When Singbonga has to be worshipped, the worship has to be performed under a Shorea robusta (sal/ sakhua tree), because it is believed that Singbonga comes down from heaven when implored and rests only on a *sarjom daru* (*sakhua* tree). Every Munda household should have a *sarjom* tree in its courtyard. *Sarhul*—the festival of flowers usually observed in spring, is the biggest festival of the Mundas during which Singbonga is worshipped in a grand way.

Mundas are monotheist, in the sense that they worship only Singbonga, the Supreme Spirit. They are not polytheist as it commonly appears when they offer sacrifices to so many *bongas* (spirits). This is not worship but is just a performance of sacrifice (offering of food and drink) to appease a particular *bonga* (spirit) who may be in need of it.

The Santal Tribe

The Santal Story of Creation

Thus goes the legend of Creation according to an oral history of the Santals, a group of the Munda race:

In the beginning there was only water and underneath it, soil. First of all, *Thakur jiu* (Supreme God), created fishes, tortoise, crocodile, earthworms, sun, moon and all kinds of living creatures of water, and finally human beings.

Out of the clay, *Thakur jiu* made forms of a human couple—Man and Woman and when He was ready to inject soul or breath (life-force) into them, the Sing Sadom (Sun-Horse) came down from above and trampled them into pieces. *Thakur jiu* was awfully pained. *Thakur jiu*, however, did not give up His plan of creating Man and Woman. Then he made the physical form of male and female birds instead of the forms of man and woman out of the damp clay and immediately imparted life breath into them from the inner part of His bosom. He named the birds 'Has' and 'Hasil' (meaning Goose and Gander). He would keep the birds on his hands and talk to them and play with them. When the birds needed a place to live, *Thakur jiu* formed the earth. The birds made a nest in a clump of thatching grass where female bird (Hasil) laid two eggs. From those two eggs two human beings—Male and Female, were hatched. They were called 'Pilchu Hadam' and 'Pilchu Buri'. Man and Woman grew up in 'Hisri Pipri'. They were taken care of by Has and Hasil—their parents, as advised by *Thakur jiu*. When the birds faced difficulty in feeding the humans, they urged *Thakur jiu* to arrange food for the two humans. *Thakur jiu* then created the fruit-bearing trees and grains. Thus, the earth and other creations on it have been created out of necessity of humans.

The first man and women lived in joy and happiness under the loving care and protection of God. They talked with Him and had fellowship with Him and knew nothing of illness and death. They did not work hard, they did not have to, because food was available everywhere and all that they did was just to collect it.

"Lita" (Chief Evil Spirit, Devil or Satan)—Santal legend does not say about Lita's origin—was unhappy when he saw the first man and woman happy and joyful. One day he visited them and introduced himself as their grandfather. Having found them in a state of innocence, he told them that they had not tasted the real joy of life. He taught them how to prepare beer and told them: "Now both of you drink this after having poured some on the ground in the name of Lita". He then left them and when he returned, he chuckled to see the change in their appearance. They had become drunken. In that condition they lost their innocence and Pride and Covetousness replaced innocence in them. Lita then taught them to make love.

Pilchu Hadam and Pilchu Budhi got children—seven sons and seven daughters. They got them paired and coupled, and the human race multiplied.

A group, branched out from the greater Munda Family of Tribes at one point of time in history, later came to be known as 'Santal'. Dr Anil Kumar in his book '*Jharkhand Me Mundaon ka Arthik Itihas*' argues that a group separated from the main Munda group at Omedanda, some 50 kilometres to the west of Ranchi when the Mundas as one race, were entering Chotanagpur after migrating from Rohtasgarh, their immediate previous inhabitat.[45] The group that separated itself there, later came to be known as the Santals.

In practice, Mundas and Santals call each other their blood kin. In the present day, the two groups live in two different geographical areas of Jharkhand. Santali language differs from Mundari only very slightly and both the languages are grouped under the same linguistic family. Roy and other scholars too, confirm that Santals are close kin of the Mundas. "The Santals are a tribe closely related to Mundas, and by far more numerous."[46]

Some scholars even call Santals as originally Kherwars, which does not seem to be true. Kherwars may have been a part of the Greater Munda Family of tribes, who probably had parted their ways even before the Santals did from the main Munda group. Presently Kherwars live in the western districts of Jharkhand.

The Santals used the term '*Horhopon*' (Sons of Man) for themselves. Later after separating from the main Munda group, they received the name 'Santal', because they settled in the land called '*Saont*' or '*Santh*' which means 'peace'. The land called Saont is in Midnapore, West Bengal[47]. Later, the Santals moved northwards and settled in what is now known as Santal Parganas.

The major concentration of the Santals is in Santal Pargana districts of Jharkhand. They also live in large number in some districts of West Bengal, Bihar and Odisha, though they can be found residing in small groups all across other Central Indian states.

According to Santal tradition, having parted ways with the main Munda group, the Santals moving by the bed of River Damodar, initially settled in Chai and Champa in modern-day Hazaribagh. From Hazaribagh, the Santals moved into Manbhum and into the Santal Parganas.

This happened during 1790s and early 1800s. The British Government formed 'Damini-Koh' following a revolt in 1832-33, after which the Santals got legal settlement from the British Government.

Singcando

The Santals name their God as 'Singcando', who is the Supreme God. They also call God as 'Thakur jiu'—which seems to be an influence of Bengali tradition as they have been living with them since long, or '*Baba*' (Father) or *Maran Ishor* (High God)[48], who is worthy to be worshipped, *'jiu'* means the Supernatural Spirit of God with characteristics of Omnipresence and Omniscience.

The Santal legend of creation may prove helpful for a better understanding of Singcando or Thakur jiu. The Santal legend of origin of humanity combines the principles of creation and evolution, for according to it humankind is ultimately derived from two images, which are modelled in human form out of damp clay. But an incident made God first create a pair of birds, from whose eggs the first Man and first Woman of flesh and blood were hatched.

'Thakur jiu' is the living God. He sees and knows the human heart. He cannot be seen with bodily eyes, but He himself sees all. He has created everything and hence is the Creator God. He keeps creating because creation is his nature. He is the Owner and Sustainer of the whole world. This name 'Thakur jiu' is descriptive of His character, His reality that he is not an abstract concept.[49] God is real to the Santals, and is spoken about and realised. He is ever present, ever acting in the real world.

Historic Santal Hul had a lot to do with the result of 'ever acting' nature of Thakur jiu—the Santals' Supreme God. Dr S.P. Sinha, former director of Bihar Tribal Welfare Research Institute (Ranchi) in his booklet 'Santal Hul' (1991) narrates the story. Sidhu and Kanhu "were at night seated in their home, resolving upon many things (in their minds); their brother Chand and Bhyrub (Bhairab), were ten miles away at Simul-chap; a bit of paper fell on Sidhu's hand and suddenly the Thakur (God) appeared before the astonished gaze of Sidhu and Kanhu. He was like a white-man though dressed in the native style; on each hand he had ten fingers: he held a white book and wrote therein; the book and with it 20 pieces of paper, in 5 batches, four in each batch he presented to the brothers; ascended upwards and disappeared. Another bit of paper fell on Sidhu's head, and then came two men each having six fingers on each hand; hinted to them the support of the Thakur's order and they likewise vanished".[50]

The Santals took the incident as order from Thakur to wield battle against the money-lenders and the corrupt British administration who protected them. Word spread that the Divinity delivered to the two brothers a sacred book, and the sky showered down slips of papers, which were secretly spread through the whole of Santal country. Each village received a scrap without a word of explanation, but with an impression that it would avoid the wrath of God, to forward it without a moment's pause to the nearest hamlet. "So from hand to hand and from village to village passed these slips of paper, apparently meaningless and vague, yet stirring the race to its depths, by their mysterious appeale with supreme force to the Santal mind"[51]. This is how Thakur jiu (God) always acts in Santal life.

Santals have rich terminology for the attributes of God which express the personal side of Thakur jiu. He is addressed as Father (*Baba*), Grandfather, Friend, but not in a human sense. They invariably refer to their dependence on God. Whether in cases of success or failure, trouble and happiness, Santals often invoke or praise, saying *'Baba Dayate'* (By the Grace of God)[52]. Thakur jiu can be angry, He can love, He can understand joy and sorrow. He hears from them and directs them in their day-to-day life. Thakur jiu has been a God of benevolence and justice, he does not tolerate injustice. He fights against injustice and liberates all from suppression and oppression and different kinds of bondage. *Thakur jiu* is obviously male in gender, and the Santhal's do not conceive a wife of this God.

Thakur jiu is also the upholder of moral law. He is the judge of humans both in this life and after death; and humans are responsible to Him for their deeds. Thakur jiu is not only believed as a judge but is considered benevolent and does not require to be propitiated by the daily offering of sacrifice. He is worshipped and offerings are made to Him in the form of thanksgiving at different occasions, like bumper harvest. Whenever everything fails, Thakur jiu is appealed to as the final court of justice, the judge of all.

Thakur jiu, being a spiritual power cannot be reduced to any form of Image and his idol cannot be made. Thus, one would not find Santals making idol of their God and worshipping Him. He is believed and understood as High Spirit. Santals worship Him, anywhere any time, as it was willed by *Thakur jiu*. He may be approached and worshipped by any person at any time and at any place. *Thakur jiu* does not exist at a limited worshipping abode, he does not need to be built a house (temple or church), for He is ever present everywhere in similar strength and power. The Santals believe that God was with humankind since the beginning of creation. He is a relational being.

The Sun

The Santals also worship the 'Sun' as the Natural Expression of the *Singcando* or *Thakur* jiu. Thus, in a sense they are Animists too. However, *Singcando* or *Thakur jiu* is not the Sun, and the Sun is only a created thing by *Thakur jiu* or *Singcando*. Therefore, it can be presumed that the original Santal ancestry knew only *Singcando*, who is the Supreme God, the all-powerful Creator God. "Among the Santals the Supreme God is identified with the natural objects, the Sun, thus He is the *Cando Bonga* or Sin Bonga (the Sun God). But the forefathers of the Santals have witnessed that the *Cando Bonga or Sin Bonga* (Sun God) is not "*Thakur jiu*". The sun is the natural object created by *Thakur jiu*"[53]. *Singcando* is thought to be fairly satisfied with the Santals and and does not put them in distress. God is the Giver, particularly the giver of the rain and if He gets displeased, famine may visit the land.[54]

The Sun-cult seems to be a development over time, borrowed probably from the Indo-Aryan religious tradition.

Bongas

The present day Santals do not recite the *Asur Kani*, the Legend of the Asurs. It is assumed that over the centuries of living separately from the main Munda group, the Santals must have unconsciously dropped this legend. However, they believe in the bonga (spirit) system, which obviously has its origin in the *Asur Kani* of the main Munda group.[55] Like the Mundas, *bonga* for the Santals is not altogether an evil spirit, and it takes care of the place where it dwells.

The *Asur Kani* also speaks of the 'parahon' (Pahan). Thus, it distinctly connotes that public sacrifices and the priests of the Singbonga existed generations before. Singbonga says: *Hatu talaren parahon sing subaren bubatukaia*. 'I shall make the village-Pahan sit under a tree (and order them to give you food)'. This order is given because after their destruction, the souls of the Asur women would become *tutelary* spirits (bonga) and be in need of food. Singbonga does not establish the pahan (i.e., create the pahanship, as a new institution), but gives them two new and necessary duties to perform, namely that sacrifice to Lutkum Haram and Lutkum Buria on the *ba*, *batauli* and *mage* feats; and that sacrifice of the tutelary spirits. At the end of the Legend, Singbonga says 'Patguru, turacelaing dotukakingtana": meaning 'before going, I shall order head-diviners and their disciples to offer and make others offer sacrifices to you so to provide food for you'.

Divination (or soothsaying), thus, seems to have been existing before the Legend. But henceforth the diviners and the soothsayers are charged with the duty to find out which spirit (i.e., souls of the Asur women) would cause harm to the people, since their purpose in doing so would be to get the food they are in need of.

There is no question, as yet, of witch-finders. It is much later that the Baranda Legend would introduce witchcraft and with it the witch-finders, the deoras and sokhas.

Thus, the conclusion that the cult of Singbonga is much older than the Asur legend, could be drawn from the fact that Singbonga is often called '*Hadam*' (The Old One). While the Mundas call Him Singbonga, the Santals call Him the *Maran Buru* (The Great Sprit). The Hos begin the sacrifice formula with the word: '*Oca Singbonga*'. In some parts of Singbhum in Jharkhand, he is called *Marang Bonga* (Supreme Spirit) by the Hos.

The Kheria Tribe

Kheria Story of Creation

The Legend of Creation, according to the oral history of Kheria, a clan of the Mundas race, goes thus:

In the beginning there was only water everywhere. There upon the waters lived Ponomoshor (*Sakhi Goshai*), Sembhu Raja and Dakai Rani. They felt empty and hence wanted to create human beings. However, they realised that before creating human beings, the Earth has to be created. Ponomoshor then churned the waters, and the waters got frozen into curd. He again churned the curd and now out of it became *ghee*. He cooked it into a flattened ghee slice and kept it in a mud vessel.

Thereafter, Ponosmohor created the water boar and ordered him: "Get inside the waters and bring up the *ghee* slice". The Water Boar dived into the waters and catching hold of it with its teeth, threw the *ghee* slice up on the waters.

Ponosmohor divided the flat ghee-slice into two, which separated the waters and formed the Earth. Ponomsohsor then wanted to create different kinds of animals to live in the waters and on the Earth. First, He created the Earthworm, then He created a Crab.

The Earth was still wet and hence Ponomoshor created the Sun and other terrestrial bodies to dry it. Now that the Earth was suitable for residing, Ponomoshor created other animals, trees and herbs, grass and leaves.

Ponosmoshor then created a white horse with wings and the horse could fly in the air. Ponomoshor took some soil and prepared idols of Man and Woman. But the flying horse would come down and kick the idols into pieces. Ponomoshor again prepared two more idols, but yet again they were broken into pieces by the flying horse. Ponosmohor got irate with this incident and prepared a rein for the horse and fashioning it on the horse he rode upon the horse. He made the horse run and run until it got so tired that it could run no longer. Thereafter, Ponomoshor prepared the idols of human beings one more time. He then placed the idols in a hole of a banyan tree. The juice from the banyan tree dripped into the mouths of the Man and Woman's idols and the two idols came into life. They slowly came out of the hole of the banyan tree and started living beside a hill. Ponomeshor then initiated them into copulation and they multiplied. Ponomoshor ordered the Man and the Woman to offer to Him sacrifices and prayers at regular intervals. Ponomeshor then created dogs to keep watch of the Man and the Woman. He then created birds of different kinds. As the human race kept multiplying day and night, the humans started becoming arrogant, selfish and greedy. They would kill the animals and birds and eat them up. After a while, they started felling fruit-bearing trees in order to collect fruit for themselves. In this act of theirs, other brethren got deprived of fruit as only the ones who came across a fruit-bearing tree fell the tree itself and took away all the fruits. Fruit-bearing trees too disappeared. Ponomeshor was very sad and He contemplated to destroy the humankind. He sent heavy rains day and night which flooded the entire earth. But some clever men went up to the hills and saved their lives.

After a while, the greed and selfishness of the human beings appeared again and felling of trees started again and became a menace. Ponomeshor this time rained fire from the sky and all the humankind got destroyed. Sembhu Raja and Dakai Rani, realised that in the rage of Ponomeshor, all the human race would be wiped out. They fetched a boy and a girl and hid the couple underneath the wet soil of the earth where the fire could not harm them.

Ponomeshor then started feeling lonely again as he no longer received sacrifices and offerings from the humans.

But when he was going around upon the Earth, he felt the odour of humans and realised that some humans were still alive. He went in search of them, thinking that He will set them up again who will progress the human race all over again. Ultimately, he found the boy—named 'Jerka' and the girl 'Jerki', who had been hidden by Sembhu Raja and Dakai Rani under the wet soil. Ponomeshor asked Sembhu Raja and Dakai Rani to give Jerka and Jerki to Him. But Sambhu Raja and Dakai Rani refused.

“You create the humans and also destroy them. And when you do not get offerings, you come looking for humans?’ Dakai Rani told Ponomeshor.

Ponomeshor regretted the display of his anger and said: “I will not destroy the humankind any more. You keep the one part of humans and I will take the other.” The one part of the human which went to Dakai Rani is the Body, and the other part that went to Ponomoshor is Soul. Thus, as long as a human being is alive, Ponomoshor has no right over his Body, and cannot destroy him. Dakai Rani and Sembhu Raja always protect the human as long as he is alive.

**

S.C. Roy calls Kherias (also known as Kharia) as part of the Munda family of tribes, sharing a common past. Kheria language, too, is very close to Mundari. The Kherias and the *Kompat Munda* (as the main Munda tribe is known) group also share similar cultural and religious practices and traditions. Kherias are 'an aboriginal tribe living in most part of Chotanagpur and akin to the Mundas, though not as closely as the Santals and other Mon-Khmers of the Ranchi plateau and Central India[56]. According to one of their traditions, an Aryan invasion drove them away from their ancestral home in North India into the wilds of Chotanagpur[57]. Presently, they are concentrated in Chotanagpur districts and in districts of Odisha, apart from parts of Chhattisgarh. According to Joakim Dundung, a Kheria scholar and author of *Kharia Jeewan aur Parampara*, Kherias are residing in states like Uttar Pradesh, Punjab, Nepal as well as in Bangladesh too[58], and continue to use Kheria language, though their customs differ from those residing in Central Indian states.

The Kherias name God as Punyomosor, which later got somewhat *sanskritised* and started being called a 'Ponomoshor', which means Self-Originated Force. Ponomoshor is believed to be root cause of the world. Ponomoshor cannot be seen in person, because he is formless—a Spiritual Force. Man can never reach Ponomoshor with his own power, he cannot see him. Therefore, the Kherias compared Ponomoshor with the Sun (*Bero or Giring*). For the Kherias, Ponomoshor is identical to the Sun, in the sense that the Sun is the biggest Force, which can ever be seen by a man; but Ponomoshor is a more powerful force that the Sun. But, in order to realise who Ponomoshor is, the Sun can be worshipped, contemplating about Ponomoshor. A Kheria believes that the blessing of Ponomoshor reaches him every morning through the rays of the Sun, and remains with him the whole day[59].

The Kherias also believe in the power of the first couple—Sembhu Raja and Dakai Rani. The couple lives in the land, particularly in the low land. They are taken as Deities—though they draw their power from Ponomoshor. These two Deities mediate between a Kheria and Ponomoshor whenever there is a gap, and it was this first couple (Lutkum Bura and Lutkum Buri of Asur Legend in Munda tradition), who saved a boy and a girl when Ponomoshor decided to rain fire upon humans who had become full of evil.

Thus, the Kheria follow a tradition with a powerful Supreme God, Ponomoshor, and other two deities—Sembhu Raja and Dakai Rani lesser in power, always playing a positive role for the Kherias, who are all born from this first couple after Ponomoshor initiated them into sex—

popularly narrated as Legend of Procreation by all the Kolarian Tribes.

Thc Log Between the Boy and the Girl

This legend is narrated at all the marriage festivals in the Kheria community and hence a popular one known by all Kheria adults. But the form in which it is being presented has been narrated by Deonis Soreng, a retired teacher of a high school in Sundergarh district of Odisha, who also holds the post of Kheria *Maha-Sohor* (Kheria Head-Chieftain of State of Odisha).

"After Ponomoshor had created everything in the world, he created a boy and a girl. The two lived like brother and sister, and they used to place a log in between when they slept at night. Ponomoshor was worried. If they continue living like brother and sister, how will the human race grow.' he thought. One day he decided to pay a visit to the boy and the girl and upon reaching their dwelling place, he called out and they answered. 'Where are the children?'—he queried the girl. 'Who? Children! We are only two, none else', the girl replied.

"Then Ponomoshor handed over the girl some herbs that he had brought along from the forest. 'Cook the rice, dry the rice on a mat and when it is completely dried, mix these herbs with the dry rice, and fill it up in a mud pot,' he instructed. 'After seven days I will pay you another visit'.

"On the eighth day, Ponomoshor arrived at the door of the dwelling place of the boy and the girl and called them out. The girl and the boy came out and welcomed him into their house. Ponomoshor ordered the girl to bring the pot out and when she did so, he instructed her to pour some water into it. A drink was ready and Ponomoshor divided it in three leaf-cups. He drank from his own and asked the boy and the girl to drink from theirs. When they had drunk the drinks, Ponomoshor took leave of them. Night fell and the boy and the girl went to sleep, placing the log in between just as other days. Ponomoshor then sent a bird which sat on the log and sang the sweetest of songs the two had ever heard. And when the song was over, it said: *'chapu, chapu'* (meaning 'touch, touch'). The boy and the girl had got drunk and when they heard words 'chapu, chapu', they threw off the log that lay in between them and touched (caught) each other.

"Thus the first marriage in the world was performed, by Ponomoshor himself; and the human race multiplied."

*

This was the only time Ponomoshor took the form of a man, and then went back to his abode in the sky. This first couple later came to be remembered as Sembhu Raja and Dakai Rani—Adam and Eve of Judaism—among the Kherias, and they keep guiding and protecting a Kheria all through his life. For the Kherias, Ponomoshor himself teaches the reluctant boy and the girl to have sex, unlike Adam and Eve of Abrahamic tradition who eat the 'forbidden Apple'.

The God of the Kherias is an Impersonal God, who took human form only once—when He visited the first couple in order to perform their marriage. Kherias believe that Ponomoshor, who lives up in the sky, resides everywhere, sees everything—and hence is also known as *Sakshi Goshai*, and also is sometimes called *Maha-Ishwar* (The Great Deity), Sembhu Raja and Dakai Rani being the other deities—the Adam and Eve, the first boy and the girl. There still are other few deities in the Kheria religious belief. To name some important ones among them, they include *Sarnapat Deota* (the deity who protects the village), *Mahadaniasarna Deota* (Protector of Humans and Cattle), *Lababah Deota, Korsuwasarna Deota, Sarhulsarna Deota, Burhisarna Deota, Bhundusarna Deota* etc. In fact, among the Kolarian tribes, Kherias probably have the highest number of deities, each protecting something or other, though all of them lesser in power than Ponomoshor, and all acting only in His permission and instruction. This is probably because Kherias happen to invent deities nearly every other day, and cook up a story for the justification of the said deity or deities. Eventually, they fall in trap of their own creation, every other day making sacrifice or offering—most of the time cocks of different size and colour— to some deity or the other. They believe that the smaller deities are created by Ponomoshor himself, for different works or protection of different things. All these deities, however, are formless and *Impersonal*—though with some *attributes*. Ponomoshor took to form once—when he came to perform the marriage ceremony of the first couple.

Thus, Kheria religious tradition, unlike Kompat Munda religious tradition, is a Polytheistic tradition. Since the Kherias also worship the Sun (*Bero* or *Giring*), the tribe is a

Nature worshipper also. A Kheria's day, in fact, begins with folded hands to the Sun standing facing the East, as soon as he sees the Sun rising. Traditionally, all of them have been early risers, because they want to catch sight of *Bero* (Sun) rising up, so that they can worship him.

The Kherias also believe in the Asur Legend, though at no public function of theirs the legend is narrated. This is because the Kherias very much believe in spirits (*Dubo*: in Kheria) formed out of Asur women (*bongas* in Kompat Munda tradition), who dwell in hills, rivulets, trees, stones, lands, uplands etc. and even offer sacrifice (food and drinks), just the way their Munda kin do, in order to appease them so that ills upon them and upon their livestock are not brought. Dubo: usually is the evil spirit—which are the Asur women's spirit. Kharias also believe in *jiyom* (spirit of the ancestors), who are good spirits and always protect and guide them. But, neither the *Dubo*: (bongas) nor the *Jiyom* (spirit of ancestors) is God and are not worshipped; they are only given sacrifice (food and drinks) for appeasement.

Ponomoshor is worshipped every morning with folded hands facing the East. But on special occasions like Bandoi (Festival of the Cattle), *Gingtang* porob (festival of the Cowshed), *Push puni porob* (harvest festival), *Jagat Puja* (Rath Yatra), etc.

Jagat (Jagta) puja—This deity originally happened to be the deity of the village that the Kherias used to worship. Gradually, this was transformed into Rath Yatra and the idol of Jagatnath or Jagarnath which got installed in Mayurbhanj and then in Puri[60].

Ponomoshor is a formless God. But he can always take form. As of now, he has taken form—so far as the Kheria tradition goes, only once. Ponomoshor is a powerful God, with kindness and anger. He can reward humans for good deeds as well as punish them, just as he did in the rain of fire, when he killed the human race who had become very evil. But, during the fire of rain, Sembhu Rani and Dakai Rani had saved one boy and one girl from death by hiding them in the pool of mud in a low land which is supposed to be where the two live. Ponomoshor, who regretted his anger and destruction of the human race, found a boy and girl hiding in the pool of mud being protected by Sembhu Raja and Dakai Rani. Sembhu Raja and Dakai Rani did not want to hand over the boy and the girl to Ponomoshor but on much of His plea, parted with the boy and the girl only after they extracted a promise from Ponomoshor that he will no longer destroy the human race.

Ponomoshor here, thus, has attributes of kindness and fatherliness. Though he is mostly a Formless God (can assume form when needed). He is a Personal God with attributes.

Ho Tribe

Baha, the Flower Story

The Earth had a beautiful daughter named Biddi. Her beauty was famed across the universe. Mother Earth had a maid who used to take care of the girl when Mother Earth went out for work. The maid would light a fire around the girl so that she could not cross the boundary to go here and there, while she did the household chores. One day the maid forgot to light the fire and got busy with her work.

Biddi on seeing some boys playing nearby went to join them. After a while she spotted a beautiful flower in a nearby pond and went into the pond to pluck it. As she was so small and did not know how to swim, she drowned.

When Mother Earth came back home, she could not find Biddi. Anxious, she ran around here and there looking for her. When she did not find her, she asked the maid:

"Where is Biddi?"

'"She was playing with the boys nearby."

'Mother Earth went to the boys and asked them: "Have you seen Biddi?"

'"She was playing with us but after some time she saw a beautiful flower in the pond and went inside to pluck it. She did not come out," said the boys.

'Mother Earth became very sad. She stopped working and spent all her time mourning the death of her daughter.

'When Mother Earth stopped working, the rains failed. All the rivers and springs dried up, and so did the plants and trees. Men and animals started to die of thirst. The men then prayed to the Almighty telling him their problem.

'The Almighty reached the abode of Mother Earth and found that she had stopped working.

'"Why have you stopped working? All of mankind is in pain."

"'Mankind is in pain! But, who will listen to my pain?" she said in tears.

"'What is your pain?"

"'My dear daughter has been snatched away by the god of Death," she said in anger.

'The Almighty set out for the abode of god of Death. On the way he found Biddi playing. He asked god of Death: "All of humankind is in pain as the Mother Earth has stopped working. You have brought her daughter here. Will you not return her?"

"'Almighty, Biddi cannot go back," the Lord of Death said.

"'Why can't she go back?"

"'Because she has eaten my grain," he explained.

"'There must be a way out. Otherwise, mankind will die out because Mother Earth has stopped working. There is no rain, the rivers and streams have dried up. Why don't you allow her to live in the world for six months and another six months with you?" Almighty suggested.

"'This arrangement is alright," Lord of Death agreed.

'Biddi came back and stayed with her mother for six months. During that time, Mother Earth was happy. Rains poured aplenty. Trees turn green. Nature swings in joy. Sarhul is the day when Biddi comes back to her mother—the Mother Earth, every year. For six months, Biddi remains with her mother and Mother Earth brings rain and greenery all over.

*

Ho tribe is an important one among the Munda Family of tribes whose concentration is mostly in the Kolhan region of Jharkhand and Mayurbhanj district of Odisha. The language and culture, legends and religious beliefs of *Ho* people are similar to that of the Mundas. "Mundas and Hos stand in the same relation as Dutch and Flemings: same race, same language, but political and geographical separation. The dialect of the Ho is scarcely different from *Hasada* Mundari, except that when in the latter a cerebral- 'd' stands between two vowels, it is generally dropped in the Ho dialect. There is much less difference between the *Hasada* and Ho dialect than between *Hasada* and *Naguri* dialect."[61] *Hasada* and *Naguri* are two forms of the same Mundari language, spoken by the same Munda tribesmen, but in two different regions. While *Hasada* is spoken in Tamar region of Chotanagpur, Naguri is spoken in Khunti-Torpa region of Chotanagpur, and the two regions are seprated only by a forest.

The Ho usually call themselves *'Ho-ko'* ('Ho' men), which is a contraction of *Hodo-ko* (*Hodo-ko*, is the word used by the Mundas for themselves, which means *men*). "The Mundas often call the *Hos* as *'Ho Mundako'* owing to their dialectical peculiarity. The Hindus and others used to call the *Hos* as *'Larka Kol'—Fighting Kols (Kol* is the word the Indo-Aryans used for all the Munda tribes, probably due to the Mundas descension from their ancient ruler Kolara), because they were too fiecre and indomitable in defending their country against the rapacity of the neighbouring chiefs, and also because of their predatory excursions. The name of *Larka Kols* still survives—the Hos do not object to it and the country they inhabit, to the South-East of Ranchi, received the name of Kolhan when it was made a different 'Government States"'.[62]

The Oraon tradition, meanwhile, says that it is their arrival in Chotanagpur which caused the exodus of the Hos. "Col. Dalton doubts this, because it is incredible that a race inferior to the Hos should have been able to drive them out. But surely, the extreme aversion of the Hos for any alien is quite sufficient to explain a free withdrawal to the large and seemingly unoccupied expanse of the jungle, the *sindisum*—the country of trees, they had before them".[63]

When the Hos moved to the *sindisum*—the country of forests, (from where comes the present name of the region *Singbhum*), they found that the region had already been occupied by the Bhuiyans, who had their own kings. The Hos lived side by side with their new neighbours in peace. But trouble arrived for them on the arrival of two Marwaris, who reached there while on their way from Jagannathpur temple, Puri. The two arrivals sought hospitality from the Bhuiyan chief and the later happily provided them with it. In days to come, the Marwaris beguiled the Bhuiayns and asked them to replace their chief with them. When the Bhuiyans did, the two Marwaris are supposed to have incited them against the Hos to expel the Hos from Chotanagpur. Struggle ensued and the Hos badly defeated the Bhuiyans and when the Marwaris saw this, they are supposed to have changed side and joined the Hos. But the Hos did not give any attention to the Marwaris.[64] In time, the Hos again moved towards what in present day is called Kolhan.

God in Ho Tribe

God, the belief system, worldview, social and religious practices of the Hos are akin to that of the Kompat Mundas in all respect. There is easy intermarriage among the Kompat Mundas and the Hos. "The Hos form one tribe with the Kompat Mundas, they speak the same language and there is no essential difference between their religious beliefs and social practices. Only the Hos have proved more refractory to the witchcraft system than the other Mundas, and they marry later in life, owing to the exorbitant price extracted for the brides".[65]

Just as the Kompat Mundas, the Ho Mundas too believe in Singbonga, the Supreme Spirit, and a host of other benevolent and malevolent tutelary bongas (spirits), who got created out of the Asur Kani when Singbonga was going up to *sirma* (heaven) after destroying the Asurs who had heated up the entire universe due to incessant iron-smelting.

The Hos believe in the Creation story that the Kompat Mundas narrate. In this, the Supreme Spirit, Singbonga, saw water and water everywhere and thought of creating the Earth. First, He created the crab and the tortoise, thinking that they will help him create the Earth. But when the two failed to help Singbonga in this noble work, He created the Earthworm, who went down to the bottom of the sea and brought mud on the top, bit by bit, eventually making the Earth. The Ho Mundas also believe in the first human couple: Luku and Lukumi. They believe in the concept of Agni-Varsha (Rain of Fire) that Singbonga carried out in order to destroy the humans who had become very wicked.

However, a pair (a boy and a girl) were saved by *Luku Burha* and *Lukumi Burhi*, from whom the humanity multiplied yet another time.

The Hos also believe in the Immortality of the Soul. They believe that the body dies and not the soul, and soon after death of a person, his soul is again born as human being in the same clan. This is why when a child is born after the death of an old man in the family, he or she is named after him or her. Usually, the children are named after the grandfather and grandmother due to this very belief in the Imortality of Soul[66].

The Supreme Spirit in the Munda group of tribes' religious tradition is all good, omnipotent, omnipresent and omniscient. As per the Asur Legend, Singbonga can take incarnation to correct ills on the earth. He is also male in gender just like God the Father in Christianity and many gods in Hinduism. Like the Hindu gods, He also has a female consort, whose nature and power is not expressed, but she plays an advisory role to Him.

There is a popular belief among people that Singbonga is the Sun God and Munda Tribes are uncompromising animists. This concept must have arisen as 'Singi' in Mundari means 'Sun' and 'Bonga' means 'Spirit'—thus 'Sun Spirit'. Singbonga is not Sun God, as has usually been mistaken, and in that sense Munda Tribes are not animists. That the Munda Tribes worship hills and rivers, lands and trees etc., is actually not worship, but appeasing the 'bongas' (spirits) that live in them by permission and order of the Supreme Deity, the Singbonga. In the Asur Legend, when he shook off the

Asur women who had clung onto him when Singbonga was flying off to heaven (*sirma*) after destroying the Asurs who were causing harm to the earth and its beings due to their greedy act of smelting iron to unnecessary amount without observing the natural laws, the Asur women had fallen off on hills and dales, rivers and fields—and these had become bongas (spirits). They needed food and if they lacked it, they had the power to cause harm. The Singbonga had given them permission to live in such things and in turn take care of them, and in return receive food from the people. But, these spirits in no way are eligible for worship—an act which is due only for the Singbonga, the Supreme God. At the most, the tutelary bongas needed only appeasement or propitiation.

This concept of Singbonga being equated with 'Sun God' must have arrived due to analogy with concepts like Ikirbonga (*Ikir* meaning 'River' and *Bonga* meaning 'Spirit'—thus *Spirit Residing in the River*), *Burubonga* (*Buru* meaning 'Hill'; thus *burubonga* meaning *Spirit Residing in the Hill*) etc; which the Asur women became after falling on ikir when Singbonga shook them off. Singbonga, thus must have been mistaken as 'Spirit Residing in the Sun' or the Sun Spirit. The word, however, is not Singi-bonga (*Singi* meaning Sun), but Singbonga. "So at first, one might think by analogy that Singbonga is 'spirit dwelling in the sun', but this the Mundas deny emphatically"[67]. In fact, when different Munda scholars were asked on the subject, they vehemently denied that Singbonga is Sun God. "Sinbonga is not Sun God. It has nothing to do with the Sun. It is the Supreme God, who created everything and who regulates everything," says

Mansingh Munda, a well-known ethno-medicine doctor and social leader of the Munda community residing in Bundu, 40 kilometres south-east to Ranchi. Bundu is famously resided by only Kompat Mundas, with a special land arrangement system called *Khuntkati*, where Mundas still are the zamindars possessing right to collect land revenue from their respective *tenants*. 'Singbonga is believed to be the Maker and the Sovereign Master of the World, the Creator of Mankind, the Master and Regulator of the Spirit World, the Provider of all goods to whom all may apply for protection, and the Avenger of evil'[68].

The tradition of Singbonga is thus monotheistic—thereby Munda religious tradition being one of the most ancient monotheist traditions of the world, much prior to traditions like Christianity and Islam, parallel to Judaism, which due to their socio-political influence are established traditions, unlike the Munda philosophical tradition which hitherto is only oral and limited to the clan itself. "In monotheist system in which Singbonga is the central figure, everything is essentially concentrated with the Munda race and their social system"[69].

That Munda tradition was essentially a Monotheistic tradition was probably all too obvious to the Mundas since long, but the culture being an oral one, this knowledge hardly became public. In the recent days however, this monotheism of the Mundas is being brought to the fore into public domain by writings. While Hoffman readily accepts in his writing of the Encyclopaedia as Munda religious tradition being that of Monotheism, scholars like Ram Dayal Munda, Rose Kerketta too—accept this[70].

In the sky, in heaven. Sirmare injgebu Singbongatana, Aking kulbulriaking pakajitana—meaning: That one who is in heaven we call Singbonga.

He wasn't Sun God but Supreme God, who dwelt in the sky. In later times, this Singbonga appears to have been identified as Sun God—singi meaning the sun, mostly in the works of non-Munda writers, which is a gross misnomer.

While the Kompat Mundas and the Ho Mundas have never come under the influence of any other non-Munda tradition, the Santhals and Kharias have. The Sun-cult of the Hindu tradition can be seen in the Kharias too, and the word 'Thakur' for Supreme God that the Santhals use is a clear influence of Bengali tradition.

❑

CHAPTER 4

Mundas and the Vedas

The Diamond Maharaja

Munda King Bhupati Rai had a store-house keeper named Birju Bhandari, who got a fort constructed for the king in Sutiambe, located to the north-east of present-day Ranchi. Occasionally, King Bhupati Rai used to travel from his palace Pabiragarh to Sutiambe fort and stay there for some days. It is during one such stay that a son named Heera was born to him. After the death of Bhupati Rai, Heera became the king.

King Heera did not give the tribute to Maharaja Durjan Sal one year. The Maharaja then sent out his soldiers to arrest King Heera, who upon learning of the coming of the soldiers, mounted on his horse and fled into the forest. The soldiers chased him for over a year and at the end managed to arrest him and bring him to the Maharaja. He was jailed. King Heera sent a diamond to the Maharaja in lieu of the tribute and asked the Maharaja to release him. The Maharaja, in order to test the purity of the diamond, called for a *luhar* (blacksmith). The blacksmith came with a huge hammer made of iron and hit the diamond with it. The diamond pierced into the iron hammer and got stuck in it. Despite tireless efforts of the blacksmith, the diamond could not be brought out. The Maharaja now sent out his soldiers to bring King Heera, who was still in jail. King Heera said that if the Maharaja did not release him he will not present himself before the Maharaja, neither will he give any clue as to how the diamond could be brought out of the iron hammer. The Maharaja released King Heera and King Heera presented himself before him. King Heera wore a huge ring made of diamond. He placed it near the diamond that had got stuck inside the iron hammer, juxtaposing the two. The diamonds attracted one another and King Heera pulled the diamond out.

Being happy with King Heera, Maharaja Durja Sal sent him off with lots of riches. King Heera then built a new capital for himself with nine forts to the south-west of Ranchi, which today is known as Navratangarh.

–As narrated in Munda Lok-kathayein

*

Lal Praveer Nath Shahdeo, a descendant of Thakur Vishwanath Shahdeo, the ruler of Barkagarh—present day Ranchi, narrates it in a slightly different way. The narration goes thus:

Ruler of Khokhra—which later came to be known as Chotanagpur (today's Jharkhand) stopped paying tribute to Mughal Emperor Jahangir. The Mughal Emperor got him arrested and put him in Gwalior Jail along with many other Rajput kings of North India. Ibrahim Khan, the Mughal army chief who raided Khokhra, took along the diamonds of the Khokhra royal family and presented them to Emperor Jahangir. One particular diamond looked different. In order to test the purity of the diamond, the Emperor called for experts. A blacksmith came with an iron hammer and hit the diamond hard with it. The diamond pierced into the hammer and got stuck in it. Despite repeated efforts, the diamond could not be brought out of the iron hammer. An official in the Mughal Emperor's court pointed out that the ruler of Heera Nagpur—as Chota Nagpur was then known as, is jailed in Gwalior and he be called to do the job.

Durjan Sal was called in. When King Durjan Sal saw what had happened, he said: "Give me just a few minutes. The diamond would be plucked out". He then took the iron hammer with his left hand and placed a finger of his right hand near the diamond that had pierced in and got stuck. King Durjan Sal wore a diamond ring on the middle finger of his right hand. The diamond ring in the king's finger and the diamond inside the hammer, attracted one another. Then the king, with a force, pulled the diamond stuck in the hammer and it came off. The Emperor asked what the matter was. "Well, the diamond that had got stuck in the hammer is a *heeri*, and the one I am wearing is a *heera*. When both are kept side by side, they attract one another, just the way a female attracts a male, and this is what happened here too. I just pulled it off".

It is here that the Mughal Emperor learnt that there is *heeri* too, and not just *heera.*

King Durjan Sal was freed and made the Maharaja of Khokhra. But when he was being freed, he asked the Emperor to release all other Rajput kings who served jail term with him in Gwalior Jail. After a few months, the Rajput royals came looking for their hero to Khokhra and when they found that he lived in a simple house in Khokhra (situated beside Bero near today's Ranchi), they called in the best mason from their kingdoms and built a nice palace for him at present day Ratugarh. Durjan Sal, now the Maharaja of Khokhra, then established marital and other relations with Rajput royals of North India.

*

Historians on Nagbanshi rulers', however, write that Emperor Jahangir doubted the purity of some diamonds that Ibrahim Khan had recovered from Khokhra during his attack and arrest of King Durja Sal. Durjan Sal, the Munda chieftain of Khokhra *('Recent researches have established that the Khokhras were Mundas and were adopted into Nagbansi tribe by their head Madra Munda.'* Reference: *Mughal Administration and the Zamindars of Bihar*, Doctoral Thesis of Tahir Hussain Ansari, Centre of Advanced Study, Department of History, Aligarh Muslim University, 2008, pg. 111 and *Bihar and Orissa District Gazetteers, Ranchi,* 1917, Patna, pp. 24-25.)

"The diamonds which Ibrahim Khan had brought from Kokrah had been given to the grinders. They were now submitted to me and among them there is one which looks like a sapphire *(nilam, the same as nilmani)*. I have not seen a diamond of a such colour. It weighs several surkhs (ratis), and my lapidaries fix its value at 3000 rupees, though they would give 20,000 for it, if it were quite white and stood the full test"—*Tuziik-i-Jahangiri, pg.* 155.

"Although, the jewellers tested the two diamonds which were brought to the emperor, they declared the best of them to be impure and the impure diamonds to be sound. Therefore, Raja Durjan Sal was recalled from the prison to judge the diamonds. He pointed out the flaw and to prove that he was right, he tied the diamonds to the ends of the horns of a ram and made the animal fight with another ram. When the diamond with the flaw split, the impurity became apparent. The other diamond remained intact. The Emperor was so pleased that he pardoned Raja Durjan Sal and released him. On being released, the Raja also begged that other Rajas who were confined in the Gwalior fort along with him should also be released. He also requested that his former position might be restored to him, including the right to sit on a chair in the presence of the emperor. These requests were fulfilled." *(Mughal Administration and the Zamindars of Bihar quotes Tuziik-i-Jahangiri, pg. 155)*

*

Munda culture, if the collective culture of the Munda group of tribes residing in Central India may be thus called, is one of the most ancient ones in the sub-continent. What began as living together in groups in plains and later in dense forests amidst wild animals, surrounded by beautiful hills and mountains, slowly took the form of god experience when they started linking the day-today experiences with a supernatural entity. Social rules came up as the individual slowly got transformed into a social being. A culture had taken shape, and this culture was centred on the 'Nature'. The culture included moral and social values, language, folklore, folktales, legends, rites and rituals, medicine etc—all of which had stood distinctively on their own, side by side with the Vedic culture. There has been rich interaction between the two cultures and who has taken what and from whom, who has borrowed what and from whom, has been a raging debate difficult to conclude with definitive outcome.

The Vedic culture, on the other hand, prides in being one the oldest cultures of the world, and Vedas being, what famous philosopher Schoupenhaur described, as 'the solace of my life and it will be the solace of my death', the 'ridicule of the fools and endless meditation of the sages'.[71] The primary meaning of the Veda is Uncreated Knowledge, Super-sensuos Wisdom. Orthodoxically, they are regarded as eternal, without beginning, unauthored. 'Either writing was unknown to them at that early period of history or they considered the words of the Vedas as too sacred to set down'.[72] While spiritually-inspired orthodox mind still believes the Vedas as authorless, philosophers cannot imagine its being authorless. They regard that the Rigveda, the first among the four and the base of all the other three Vedas—Sam, Yajur and Atharva, was composed by poets who were great seers, whose names were household words even before there were households. "Another anachronistic idea is that Vedas are apauruseya, 'of non-human origin. They never regard themselves as such. The idea comes from Purva Mimamsha, a philosophical system that arose several centuries after the end of the Vedas. The Rigveda was composed by poets, human individuals whose names 'were household words even before there were households. *Viswamitra* (Friend of All), *Bharadvaja* (Bearing Strength), *Dirghatamas* (Seeing Far into Darkness)'.[73] However, on one thing all agree: that the Vedas are embedded with priceless spiritual, philosophical and worldly insights, and this must certainly have taken deep intuition of the seers, who still being in this very world, transcended to the other to draw insights from, who could stay connected with this wordly life and still remain one with the Transcendence, in a way to make people feel that their words were not theirs, but that of the Unseen Power so sublime, and that their lips were just Material Cause and not the Efficient Cause.

While the Rig Veda is supposed to be the oldest so inferred because of its 'language which is archaic, and because the other three Vedas presuppose, depend on, quote or refer to it',[74]—mainly dealing with hymns in praise of different deities. 'Many of its invocations ask god for long life, riches, sons, cattle and victory in battle. They discuss sex with the same attention to detail as rites. They contain speculations about universe and much else.'[75] Atharva deals with spells and incantation. 'Instead of poets, singers or priests, we meet with physicians and magicians who use drugs and spells to cure diseases, mental as well as physical.'[76]

One finds mention of the word 'Munda' in the Rig Veda several times[77], and about '300 words that occur in the Rigveda are not Indo-Aryan or Indo-European but come from elsewehere. Many have come from Munda, a group of languages still spoken in parts of India, a proto-Munda'[78]. Munda belongs to the large group of Austro-Asiatic languages that include Khmer, Mon, Vietnamese and sevety-five others in South-east Asia[79]. That 'the indigenous population contributed substantially to the Vedas follows from the fact that the names of indigenous families, clans and tribes, became the names of Vedic schools (*sakha*).... These units had no chieftains, not to mention of bishops; but there were experts (*brahmanas*) of the language (*brahman*) who included members of the indigenous groups that had started using Vedic as a second, third or another language'[80]. The Samveda undoubtedly came from 'an indigenous, non-Indo-Aryan lineage. With the Yajurveda, composing Vedas became something like a job. The Atharva is replete with local cults'[81].

However, gradually there may have been not just cultural, but marital intercourse too, between the two races of people and a new society evolved. The Aryan group cannot have contributed more than a few Y-chromosomal lineage'[82] as most were men, and they married local women. As it happens, the woman being the master of the household in practical sense, many elements of culture that the woman inherited from her society slowly got adopted by the Aryan men and their new households. The Vedic people had the 'language', and the Rigveda testifies it when it says: 'Soma unpressed has never elated Indra, nor its pressed juices unaccompanied by sublime language'[83]. The heritage of powerful 'language' (or words) of the Vedic people was the basis on which Veda itself rested. It is a tradition that stressed more on 'how you say what you say' rather than just the 'what'. Language is the gateway to the World, and with this 'language' (words), the Vedic people created a web of knowledge. The belief that there must have been furious battles between the Indo-Aryan and the Austro-Asiatic races (or the Dravidian race), is not accepted by many scholars today. 'The tribals [here the Indo-Arynas] did not invade or conquer, as has long been assumed. They mingled and settled with others already there. There were battles as well as alliances, the latter between the tribes as well as persons.'[84] The passage in the Vishnu Puran: I 5: 28-32, describes the Asuras as the first born of the Brahman, from whom they sprang; and the similar statement in the Mahabharata that the Asuras were the elder brothers of the gods—and further statements in the Taitreya Upanishad (VI.2), that formerly the Earth belonged to the Asuras while the gods had only as much as a man can see while sitting, are of relevance. There are many hymns in the Rigveda in which we hear the fair-skinned Aryan warriors invoking the aid of their bright and beneficent gods against these and other black races who long and strenuously fought—and fought in vain—to stem the tide of Aryan progress in the country.

Vedic Gods

Man's quest for someone of whom he came into being—by going back in time—who created the things that he saw and found around him, has been since the beginning of time. When he found order and harmony in the creation in all that he saw and found, his quest for the Creator became even more intense. It is difficult to fathom how the first

'Homosapien'—if we go by the Evolution Theory of Charles Darwin—must have reacted when he had started thinking with reason, coming of age from the less thinking or even non-thinking predecessor. He must definitely have wondered at the creation all around him and then sat down to think: 'If his existence is a reality, how did he come into being?' If the Creation, in which he found Order, is real; then where did it all come from? And when he saw a child getting born from sexual intercourse with his partner, beaming with life and vivacity, he must definitely have wondered where did the child get life from? Did he give the life to the child? Or someone else? But this stage of intense thinking must definitely have arrived later. It has been a long-standing belief of thinkers and philosophers, that mesmerised by the power of different things in the Nature, man took them for gods, because anything which is 'powerful' was certain to be taken as 'god' by him.

It is pertinent to note here that the PURUSHA SUKTA—Purusha meaning 'Cosmic Man',[85] which is taken to be the root justifying the pantheon of Vedic gods:

'A thousand heads had Purusha, a thousand eyes, a thousand feet.
He covered earth on every side,
and spread ten fingers' breadth beyond.

The Purusha is all that yet hath been and all that is to be;
The lord of immortality which waxes greater still by food.
So mighty is his greatness; yea, greater than this is Purusha.
All creatures are one-fourth of him,
three-fourths eternal life in heaven.

With three-fourths in Purusha went up: one-fourth of his,
again was here.
Then he strode out on every side over what eats not and what eats.

From his Viraj was born; again Pursuha from Viraj was born
As soon as he was born he spread eastward
and westward o'er the earth.

When gods prepared the sacrifice with Purusha as their offering,
Its oil was spring, the holy gift was autumn; summer was the wood.

They balmed as victim on the grass Purusha born in earliest time.
With him the deities and all Sandhyas and Rishis sacrificed.

From that great general sacrifice the dripping fat was gathered up.
He formed the creratures of the air, and animals both wild and tame.

From that great general sacrifice Richas and Sama-hymns were born:
Therefrom the metres were produced, the Yajus had its birth from it.

From it were horses born, from it all creatures with two rows of teeth:
From it were generated kine, from it the goats and sheep were born.

When they divided Purusha, how many portions did they make?
What do they call his mouth, his arms?
What do they call his thighs and his feet?

The Brahman was his mouth,
of both his arms was the Rajanya made.
His thighs became the Vaisya, from his feet the Sudra was produced.

The moon was generated from his mind,
and from his eyes the Sun had birth.
Indra and Agni from his mouth were born,
and Vayu from his breath.

Forth from his navel came mid-air;
the sky was fashioned from his head;
Earth from his feet, and from his ear the region.
Thus they formed the worlds.

Seven fencing-logs had he, thrice seven layers of fuel were prepared,
When the gods, offering sacrifice, bound, as their victim, Purusha. [86]

*

According to the Vedas, Brahman manifested a part of Himself during creation and diversified Himself into Isvara, Hiranyagarbha and Viraj. He created the earth, the mid-region, the heaven. He created gods and celestial beings, demons and humans/ God and celestial beings reside in the heaven and the mid-regions respectively. Humans and other mortal beings inhabit the earth or our world. The demons reside in the nether regions below the earth. In the mortal world, He manifested as Death (or Kala) and became its ruler. He created hunger and thirst and subjected the beings, including the gods in the heaven to the same. To satisfy them He created food of several kinds. The gods have immense powers, but they do not have the ability to make food for themselves. Human beings have the ability to make food for themselves and others, but do not have the supernatural powers of the gods. Brahman created this distinction to ensure that both gods and humans live in harmony, depend upon each other, and participate in creation by doing their duties. Thus, it is the duty (*dharma*) of gods to help humans and it is the duty (*dharma*) of humans to live helpfully and help gods and other beings with nourishment by performing sacrifices.

Gods in Macrocosm and Microcosm

The Vedas declare that the human body is similar to the body of the Cosmic Self, Purusha, who manifested in creation as the Lord of the Universe. Through the sacrifices and invocations, the worshippers of the Vedic gods sought wealth, peace, happiness, progeny, fame and name, power over the natural forces, destruction of enemies, longevity or a full lifespan, good health, protection from misfortune, sickness and loss of cattle. Over the time, many gods and deities came to be established in Vedic religious tradition, each with personal attributes of specific kind. These gods and deities were worshipped on different occasions. Rigveda is usually in praise of all these deities, who are offered prayers and oblations seeking wealth, power, fortune, sons and other worldly and heavenly things

In the Brihadaranyaka Upanishad[87], when Vidadgha Sakalya asked Yajnavalkya, how many gods were there, he began the answer by saying, "As many are mentioned in the Nivid of the Visve-devas—three hundred and three, three thousand and three." On being queried further, Yajnavalkya reduced the number gradually from three thousand three to thirty-three, then to six, then to three, then to two, then to one and half and finally to one. In the same conversation, he identified 33 gods as the important ones, namely eight Vasus, eleven Rudras, twelve Adityas, Indra and Prajapathi Brahma. These gods belong to different sphere in creation.

Shiva and His Son

Munda tribesmen have rich and first-hand knowledge of the wildlife, flora and fauna; living as they have been in their midst since ages. They seem to understand the language of the nature and the wild animals; and Nature and wild animals reciprocate. Visits to forest-villages in Central Indian States inhabited by tribes would reveal that they have a mine of knowledge of the wildlife and flora and fauna that awaits to be documented and scientifically verified. It is their wildlife knowledge that helps them tackle simple and complicated situations that may arise by way of man-animal conflict, which has become all too frequent in recent days due to obvious reason of massive deforestation and ecological imbalance. The author came across some interestring stories about how Munda and other tribesmen of forest-villages have tackled situations of man-animal conflicts. Elephants, which a mythical story terms 'Munda by origin', are at the centre of several true stories.

Koilsar, Night of July 15, 2016

The village is called Koilsar, located on the borders of Jharkhand and Odisha beside a forest. A group of elephant experts which styles itsef as 'Hathi Kheda' is in high demand all around the region as man-elephant conflicts is all too common. Marianus Kerketta, who is the head of the Hathi Kheda, has many stories in his kitty that forms part of his about two decades' personal experience with elephants, one of the most unpredictable animals of the world, worshipped as a deity Ganesha, the son of Shiva, by many. Marianus pulls out two stories and narrates—as being told hereafter—and at the end also reveals some innate Munda knowledge about elephants.

*

That night, Dilu's wife Rita, a mother of three, was sleeping in her portion of a huge house owned by the family. Her husband wasn't home and children studied in cities elsewhere. The house had two portions, in the other slept her in-laws.

It was around midnight when my cell phone rang. I usually keep my cell phone on the whole night. I picked up the call and from the other side came a feeble voice: 'Where are you? Some elephants have come in to my courtyard.' I recognised the voice. It was Dilu's wife, my sister-in-law. 'I am here in the house itself. Don't worry,' I said. My house was next to her courtyard. In fact, we shared our boundaries. And the elephants were behind my own house, in the courtyard of Dilu.

Dilu's courtyard had a jackfruit tree which had lots of fruits that year. July is the month when jackfruits ripen. Elephants loved jackfruit. I understood they had come looking for jackfruit straight inside the backyard of Dilu, behind my own house. 'Marianus, everyday you chase elephants from others' courtyards and houses. It is time to take care of your own backyard,' I said in mind, as I kept the cell phone conversation on. 'What do I do?' my sister-in-law asked. Her voice suggested that she was very afraid and did not know what to do.

I quickly uttered the '*names*' of my five fingers in Mundari. This was to ensure that the elephants do not come to the place where I am put. I also chanted the mantra. Then I called out in soft voice, in my own mind. The elephant responded with an *aunnn*...sound. I immediately knew he understood that I am here, nearby by. Then I took some names (I would desist from revealing them for some reason). After that I lit the *mashal* (fireball) and came out of my own house softly. I ventured towards my own backyard, the courtyard of Dilu. I saw four huge elephants, after breaking the huge iron-gate of the boundary of Dilu's house, had entered in the courtyard. One was plucking the jackfruits and throwing them on the ground for the rest three to eat.

'*Jome pe* (Eat),' I said. I did not disturb them, for they were hungry and needed food. When the elephants are hungry and thirsty, one should not disturb them. They should be allowed to eat and drink. I then dialled the number of Raju, a colleague in our *Hathi Kheda* group. His house is located about half a kilometre away from mine. 'Elephants are in my backyard. Come with your fireballs,' I told him. Meanwhile, I also called up a few more youths of the village. Elephants do not go away if they see only one or two men. You require at least four men in the group, each with fireballs, to send elephants away. Raju and other youths came from different directions with fireballs in a while.

'*Dola hora hora te* (Let's go, take the path),' I uttered in Mundari loud enough, so as to make my voice audible to the elephants. One of them stopped eating and looked towards me. I was still holding the fireball and fellow youths of my group and others from the village too had gathered there with their own fireballs. '*Dola hora hora te,*' I repeated, this time a little louder. The other three elephants too stopped eating. In fact, they had finished eating, finished nearly all the jackfruits from the tree. '*Dola dola. Jompa re dola*' (Move,

move. Move towards your right side), I said. Towards their right was the iron-gate that they had broken open and got inside the courtyard. Now, all of them raised their trunks towards us. I understood that they had eaten their share and were happy. When elephants raise their trunks, it is a sign that they are happy and they are saying goodbye to you, ready to depart. They started moving to their right. Slowly, they went out of the boundary of the house and moved towards the field. We went behind them, all with our fireballs. Elephants are afraid of fire.

After a while when we reached the paddy field, to our horror, we found that a large number of elephants were feasting on the paddy growing on the field of Dilu. They were probably more than 15 in all, each of different size. They had grazed nearly everything. There too, we allowed them to eat to their hearts content. And after a while we repeated the same directives that we had issued for the four big ones that had entered Dilu's courtyard. We chased them all to the nearby forest and came back home.

On the following morning, we when I went to the rice field, I counted at least sixteen elephants' feet. We count their numbers by different foot size that they leave behind on the ground. Dilu, who had come back home in the morning after a night duty, joined us in counting the foot size. Since then, it became a 'Dilu story' of elephants. We name the story by the owner of the house where the incident took place.

*

Dahijeera, Day of March 25, 2018

This story is narrated by Raju, nephew of Marianus—

Dahijeera is about 10 kilometres away from Koilsar, also on the borders Jharkhand and Odisha. Mostly agrarian tribal people reside in the village. The village is surrounded by rivers and huge tracts of agricultural fields that produce varieties of rice and green vegetables.

After my breakfast—which consists of rice cooked on the previous night and some fresh vegetables, I picked up my axe and my bow and arrow to go to the forests to collect *mahua* (maduca latifolia). My cell phone rang. I picked up. It was an unknown number but I expected an elephant call.

'Am I talking to Raju Kerketta?', said a young man, in a hurried voice. 'Yes, yes,' I said. 'Elephants have come into the village. Please rush to our aid with your squad'. 'Where are you calling from?' I inquired. The boy in a hurry had not bothered to mention the name of his village. I was cool because such calls have been regular for the last ten years. 'Okay, we are coming. It will take about an hour for us reach. Till then, do not try to go close to the elephants, and do not tease them,' I warned the man.

That day, the vehicle, an open jeep we used for rushing to the incident spots, was coincidentally parked near my house. I called the other members of our squad. As soon as they arrived with the instruments we use to send away elephants—usually fireballs attached to long iron rods that is fitted to a long strong *lathi*, we jumped into our open jeep and set off.

It took us an hour's drive to reach Dahijeera. When we reached there, it was already around 10 in the morning. The villagers informed us that as many as 35 elephants had descended into the village from the nearby forest. Before they entered the village, they had bath in the nearby rivulet; they played *jal krida*—how this 'krida' is played would come later—in it. And they marched towards the village.

'They are in the village for the last four hours. They have already broken six houses and eaten the food grains from those houses,' said a man who introduced himself to us as Aman. It was Aman who had called me on my cell phone. We, the five members of our *Hathi Kheda* squad mapped the situation, after which it was decided that we should focus the lead female. Usually, it is elderly female who is the boss of the herd and all others, including the male tusker— who usually likes to remain aloof, does what she does. As usual, each one of us took the names of the five fingers of our hands. In my mind, I chanted the Mundari *mantra* used for such occasion. Apart from me only my uncle Marianus knows the elephant *mantra* while other members of the squad are yet to be disclosed of it. We then lit up our fire balls even if it was broad daylight and headed towards the female boss. It had entered into the courtyard of a house and was pulling down the tiles of the roof. She had already done with other houses too, and probably had eaten enough. I took the *'names'* that we take before addressing the elephants, and said, *'Dola hora horate te'* (Go, start moving on the path) in Mundari. She did not respond. *'Dola hora hora te,'* I raised my voice a little and directed for the second time. I had expected that she would start moving away. But instead, she straightened her ears.

I sensed trouble. She moved towards me, I moved a foot towards her. She stopped. If an elephant straightens his or her ears, know that she is getting angry with you. And if she or he starts running towards you, you must move a foot forward. If you run back, she will know that you do not know her, and she will come charging you. As elephants are very fast runners, it is practically impossible to save yourself by running away unless there is a place of safety to protect yourself. I commanded her again. But it had no effect on her. For the first time during my ten years of chasing elephants I witnessed that an elephant had disobeyed me. In no time, she reached where I stood with other members of my squad beside me; caught my right arm and threw me away. I fell down on the ground. She charged towards me again, but meanwhile two of my fellow members gathered courage and pushed the piercing iron head with the fireball attached to it, into her ears. They drove her away from me. Meanwhile, we kept repeating the names that we take, and the commands in Mundari that we utter. She retreated. She took her path and started moving away. I had got up from the ground. I heard her giving out a shrill sound as she moved. Other members of the herd too, started following her.

That day was the most dangerous day of life in my self-chosen social service career.

As the herd started moving away, the villagers who were behind us, joined us forming a bigger crowd. They waded through the rivulet and walked towards the forest. The entire exercise took us four long hours. At the end of it, I had no words on my lips. The vivid pictures of the female elephant catching me by my right arms and throwing me on the ground still haunted me. But, I do not regret going to Dahijeera. Had I not gone there with my squad, the angry elephants would surely have caused some mishap with the innocent villagers.

*

Ambapani, August, 2015

The five members of the *Hathi Kheda* group reached Ambapani, another neighbourhood forest on an August afternoon. A herd of elephants had killed a villager there. The villagers called the Hathi Kheda a day after the incident. What made them call a day after? 'They had to call us because the elephants continued to be around the village even after they had killed a man. In fact, they came back to the village the night after the man had been killed, and cried in loud voice,' recalls Gautam Lakra, another member of the group.

From their village, it took the group two hours ride to reach Ambapani, situated virtually on a hill top, surrounded by dense forest all around.

'When we reached there, the villagers were busy preparing for the burial of the dead man. They told us that the elephants are nearby and they may come back again tonight too. They could not understand why the elephants weren't going away though they had already caused a casualty and destroyed quite a few houses,' Gautam recalls.

Even for the elephant-men it was a new experience. They did not have an answer to the question of the villagers—'why weren't the elephants going away?'

'We decided to stay back in the village'. The night after they committed the killing, the elephants had come back. They had caused no harm to men; neither had they destroyed any house. They did cry the whole night around the village. That's all they did! Tonight too, as all signs pointed, they had made up their mind to come back. But why?—the elephant-men had a mystery to uncover and it thrilled them. The group had braved many dangerous situations on earlier occasions, but this situation was filled with suspense and mystery. The group did not exactly know the minds of the elephants or what was going to unfold.

The family had not been able to bury the victim as it was waiting for relatives to arrive. Some relatives lived far away in cities. The family therefore had decided that it would be burying the dead only when they arrive. They were supposed to arrive only on the third day. The dead body of the victim had been kept in his house itself while the villagers that day dug the grave and readied it by afternoon. Among the tribal people, the usual practice is one of burial. The relatives arrived. At around four in the afternoon, the victim was laid to rest in the graveyard. The village has a community *masna* (graveyard). After burying the dead, villagers went to the nearby rivulet for ritual bath, and took oil and turmeric. Villagers huddled at one place as they were still apprehensive that the elephants might come back and cause further harm. Night had overtaken and just as apprehended, they elephants cry could be clearly heard now. The villagers and the elephant-men got alarmed. They did not know what the elephants were upto and hence did not know how to face the situation. Last night too, the herd had behaved in the same odd manner.

'Our fireballs were ready. The villagers too had prepared some fire balls on their own. We lit up all of them and proceeded to the border of the village. The trumpet came from the direction where the *masna* of the village lay; where the victim had just been buried. We stood ready with our fireballs lit. It was a kind of trumpet we heard for the first time in life—it felt that the elephant(s) which gave out the cry was/were in some kind of an utter disturbance. When we found that they did not venture into the village, we decided to relax. The night passed peacefully. On the following morning when the elephant-men, along with other villagers, visited the burial place of the victim, they were completely perplexed. To their dismay they found that the herd went there in the night when the villagers slept. They also saw additional heaps of soil on the tomb. 'This was indicative for us to guess that the herd went to the tomb in order to lament and perform the last rites of the victim. They were only waiting for the body to be buried in the tomb so that they could perform the last rites,' says Marianus. The elephant-men said to the villagers that the elephants may again turn up at the tomb at night, and hence issued instruction to place some oil and turmeric on some plates. 'We wanted to see whether the elephants purify themselves with oil and turmeric,' Marianus says.

Two days later, the elephant group received a phone call from Ambapani again. 'That night too, the elephants went to the burial place, and did the oil and the turmeric ritual before they departed into deep forest. We thus added yet another piece of knowledge about elephants', Marianus says.

*

Elephant, Elephant and Elephant

The elephant-men were happy to share their knowledge that they had acquired over years about this huge being. For the tribal people residing in forest-villages, he elephant is an animal that signifies lots of fellow-feeling, love and joy, with a restless wandering for food and water. It is during this wandering that they come in contact with humans and reveal a bit about their lifestyle and worldview.

To the tribesmen residing in the forests bordering Jharkhand-Odisha, it is still a mystery why the elephants understand Mundari language. Though the myth of the young Munda woman turning herself into a huge animal that later came to be known as 'elephant' followed by her own Munda husband in the same form, stretches too far into mere conjecture, the *'mantras'*, *'names'* and directives all issued in Mundari language by the *Hathi Kheda* elephant-men, as claimed, has been consistently worked for decades. The Mundari sentence—*Dola hora hora te* (go on your path) has worked. If the elephant comes charging, they say—*'Tingu me'* (stop!). And if he or she still does not stop, they say—*'Auri tingu me'* (stop there!). And the elephant stops. If the elephant has to be directed to go to his right, the men say—*'jom pa re dola'* (go to your right!) and if he or she has to be directed to the left, they say—*'lenga pa re dola* (go to your left!). If the men have to direct the elephant to turn and go back, they say—*'ruar me, ruar me'* (go back, go back!). If the elephant is eating something, it should not be disturbed; it should be allowed to eat, for food is his need just as it is for humans. In fact, at some places, the men take them to paddy fields just to feed the, saying—*jom me* (you eat!).

The *'name'* that the elephant-men referred to (they do not like to reveal!) may be related to the original name of the woman, who, in the mythological story, turned into an elephant; or the father-in-law of the woman. This (or these) name(s) is taken before the elephant to convey the message to him or her that the men 'know' him or her. Then comes the 'mantra' (this too the men do not like to reveal!). All that they say is this *mantra*, which has to be recited in low voice, is used to ensure that the elephant does not come close to people. This *mantra* probably is the one that the elephants' caretaker (*unseen caretaker*, as we will see later) uses to herd them. They also talk of 'names of five fingers in Mundari' (this too they do not like to reveal!). The names of five fingers of one's hand is taken, according to the men, is to ensure that the elephant does not *dare* to harm you. If it still harms, he or she may actually be 'outcaste' from his or her community for life. For extra protection, the men also carry some herb in their pockets that dispels elephants, and the elephants like to run away from.

In a herd, the eldest female is the boss. She leads the way, and the rest in the herd will follow what she does. The tusker will walk at the end in the herd. Interestingly, this habit of the elephants is purely Munda by character. Often, in peacetime the tusker will keep aloof, walking at the end of the herd, without bothering to take care of the other members. Often the chasers, in case the tusker at the end of the herd is too careless, leave him to his own freedom and egg the rest on. In that case, the tusker will reach the destination taking an alternative route, before the herd manages to reach, and welcome them. Children are the most loved in the herd, and the elders literally protect them from public view in order to make doubly sure that not a scratch befalls on them. If a bridge comes on their way, they will not walk through it. They come back and take a way underneath the bridge, even if there is a river to cross. While crossing a river, the female will be at the head and the second one will catch her, and all others will catch one another. At no cost they separate. If someone—except the main tusker, is left behind, the entire herd comes back. If the herd splits into two, first group will come back to the second.

A running elephant can stop in a split of the second, and its braking system works better than a hydraulic brake of a luxurious high-end car. If it straightens its ears, trouble is in the offing. If it kicks the earth with its front legs, it is angry. It may make a gud..gud.. (vroom...!) sound, just like the sound of a vehicle when it's engine is switched on.

The elephant also makes a crying sound when it is sad. It makes this sound particularly when it does some harm to innocent humans, like killing a man in a fit of rage. If an elephant kills a man without any crime on the part of the man, and does not repent or take part in the last rites of the man, he or she gets outcasted by the rest of the herd. He or she would have to spend the rest of his or her life alone, wandering alone. It is this kind of elephants which prove to be dangerous, as they literally have lost their heads because of lack of acceptance by their community. An elephant cannot live a happy life being single, it is a social being; individualism is not in its value-system. The herd will at no cost desert a member in danger; it will try to bring the victim out of danger before moving to another place. A child in danger will never be left to its fate.

The elephant's trunk is its radar. It uses its trunk to sense food and water—which it can do for nearly an area of three-kilometre radius. It raises its trunk in the air in order to sense where food and water is available. Then it proceeds exactly in that direction. Even when it breaks open houses in villages, it breaks the wall of thatched houses at exactly the spot where the rice pack is placed inside the room. But it does so only in a case when food is not available outside. In normal case, it likes to eat its food available in the open. After the elephants have eaten to their hearts' content, they raise their trunks in a posture of blessing and give out a happy sound before walking away.

Dogs are the enemy of the elephant. The elephant chasers keep the dog away when they are at work. The bark of a dog can drive an elephant nuts. It starts chasing the dog and if in the process the dog enters a house, the elephant follows in. The enmity of the elephant with the dog is not just mythical.

A wild elephant, however, is afraid of a horse. The chasers have experienced that if a herd is being driven away and on the way a horse whinnies, the elephant abruptly stops, takes a U-turn and runs.

Elephants love water. If they are moving from one place to another and find a pond or a waterbody with lots of water, they will enter it. They play *jal krida* with lots of joy and happiness. It is in the water that they copulate. And the entire duration lasts anywhere between two to three hours. During this time, they like no disturbance, and the chasers ensure that they are not disturbed. Usually, a male elephant attends to two-three females. If any female has not availed satisfaction, she is free to find a male separately. In this case, she stands on an upland, say a hill top; and gives out a long *aunggg*...sound. The male on the other end will respond with a similar sound. The female will wait for him on that particular place until the male comes and finds her. Then the couple will rejoin the original herd of the female, and the herd will accept the new member with lots of celebrations like throwing mud on each other. If a group has more male members than females, the male is free to look for a female. In this case, the male gives the first call and the female responds to him. The male waits for his female until she finds him; and the two then rejoin the original herd of the male. Thus, the elephants are both matrilineal and patrilineal. The family of a senior female and senior male—the great grandparents, consists of members numbering anywhere between 20-35 baby and adult elephants. If the family becomes bigger than this, this splits into two. There again, the leader of the new group is the second oldest parent of the original group next to the senior most parents from the group. The elephant-men have never seen any wild elephant getting old and dying a natural death. Even in the forests, news of natural deaths of elephants is nil. Forest dwellers who literally live with wild animals, have never found any dead body of an old elephant in the forest. Deaths, however, occur to elephants due to accidents like lightning, train accident, electrocution, fall in wells or by injury. It is therefore still a mystery whether wild elephants die a natural death at all!

A few years ago, a mysterious incident took place in Bamda, a dense forested region of Odisha—which incidentally is a favoured home of wild elephants. Bamda had been a princely state of ruled by the branch of Nagbanshi rulers of Chotanagpur. The Nagbanshi rulers have basically been Munda by descent, and in Bamda too a large number of Munda population resides. Bamda Nagbanshi rulers have family relationship with Chotanagpur Nagbanshi rulers even today. One day, a female elephant that had entered a village in search of food and water, was shot by some gun men. The bullet pierced her right leg and severely wounded her. She, however, managed to flee the place into the forest. She was shot in the morning and in the evening some villagers of a forest village, who were out there roaming about, spotted a peculiar sight with her. Beside her stood a man in a tribal attire, and taking some ointment from his *tumba* (a pumpkin vessel used for carrying liquid, like water and medicine) and applying it on the wounded portion of her leg. When he spotted the Munda villagers, he disappeared and could not be seen any more. The elephant also ran away in a lightning speed. However, the man, in a hurry, could not pick up the *tumba* that he had placed on the ground while treating the wounded elephant. The Munda men went near the place and picked up the *tumba* to see what it contained. They found a liquid like medicine inside the *tumba*. They went back home with the *tumba* along. On the following morning, they looked for a villager with wound so that they could test and see for themselves what the medicines were for. They applied the ointment on the wound of the villager and, to their surprise, saw that the wound healed completely within a few minutes. According to the men of *Hathi Kheda* squad, elephants have caretakers who are basically spirits (*bonga*). If a wounded elephant manages to reach her 'area', the caretaker takes care of her wound, and howsoever it may have been injured, the wound is definitely going to be healed once medicine is applied. In fact, the *Hathi Kheda* group reveals that there are spirit caretakers for each kind of wild animals, particularly wild boars and elephants. No animals will die of a wound if they manage to reach the place of their spirit caretakers. The Bamda villagers, after testing the ointment of the spirit caretaker of elephants, tried to find out what herbs it contained, but could not know what was there in the medicine.

If there are many tuskers in a group, they often fight among themselves, probably for supremacy in the group. When fight ensues among them, it is no less than a scene of an action film. The tuskers hit each other with their trunks. If they find trees, they uproot them and hit each other with them. During this time other members of the herd do not come near. They watch only from a distance. The fight lasts anywhere between an hour to two. The fight ends only after the supremacy issue is settled. If the fight takes place near a village, villagers should flee the place, for the fighters do not understand any language. Issue of ego too causes a fight. Sometimes, two groups of elephants may take to fight. This kind of fight is usually for sway over a particular area. If such a fight begins, the entire forest or forest village becomes a battle ground of elephants. While fights among two tuskers are common, fights among two groups of elephants are rare.

Elephants roam about basically for two reasons: food and water. With forest land fast depleting, their home has been robbed off. Rivers and rivulets in the forests are drying up and this is too painful for elephants. Elephants need a lot of water in rivulets and waterbodies of forests in order to play and procreate. When they reach a village looking for food and water, they actually go there to claim their right to existence, as food and water in their habitat—the forest, is running out. After they have eaten their share from the field or the house of a villager, all of them raise their trunk in joy and say: 'We have eaten our share and we are leaving your share of the crop or food grain. Next year we will come again'. In fact, the size of crop yield of a field from where elephants eat, gets bigger than normal yield that particular year.

Shiva

The complete tribal nature and behaviour of Shiva makes one wonder whether he forms part of the pantheon of Vedic gods. His living style, his love for mountains and reptiles and his carefree nature resembles a Munda more than a Vedic man. Interestingly, while 'Shiva' does not find mention in the Vedas, the tradition of worship of Shiva (or Mahadeo) is very much entrenched in the Munda culture. It is believed, as mentioned earlier, that Shiva was the one who officiated the first marriage of the first Munda boy and the Munda girl. The three drank *'rice beer'*, a drink prepared by the girl using the tips and herbs supplied by Mahadeo—Mahadeo is believed to be the teacher of herbal medicine. He then sent a bird which sang the sweetest of song to initiate the first couple into sex. And when the first couple found that a child was born after nine months, the two, now husband and wife, attributed it to the 'power' of their sexual organs, collectively taken as one. They started worshipping the *Linga* and the *Yoni*, and as Shiva was the one who had officiated in all this, later this culture developed in the form of worship of Shivalinga. This is the reason why a young Munda girl at marriage is gifted with *shilot-lodha* (a set of grinding stones that resemble like *linga and yoni*), symbolically meaning thereby that the new couple now is socially sanctioned for sex.

'Shiu' is a common name among Munda youths. The word '*shiu-tana*, a verb in Mundari, means to 'plough', which has two meanings: i) to till the agricultural land (Earth), and ii) to have sex. When a boy gets married and starts living with his new wife, his friends ask: *'Besgi shiu-tanam chi*?'—are you ploughing well? And he will chuckle as he understands the meaning. Just as ploughing bears fruit in terms of paddy and other food grains, the sexual meaning of the verb bears fruit in terms of a child.

Interestingly, *'shiu-tana'* (to plough) is a complete masculine verb. A woman is not allowed to plough in the Munda group of tribes because the earth is taken to be feminie in gender, and ploughing by a woman would amount to lesbianism, which is barred in the group. Even in the new age when tractors have replaced ploughs, a Munda woman is not allowed to drive a tractor to till an agricultural filed.

Though the word 'Shiva' does not find mention in the Vedas, is 'Rudra', the Vedic god synonymous to him? The

Rudra of the Rigveda is a god of storms and lightning. Rudra enjoyed his own importance in the Vedic pantheon because of his tempestuous nature, his association with storms and storm gods called Maruts and his ability to bring medicines to the people to prolong their lives.

Surya

War with the Sun

Several years back when many popular gods of today were not born, an Asur king named Logundi ruled his Asur kingdom. He had a beautiful daughter Jara and when the Sun saw her one morning as she bathed in a river, he went crazy about her beauty. The Sun grew lustful day by day and one day decided to snatch away the girl from her father. Knowing the ill intention of the Sun, king Logundi married off his daughter with the son of his lieutenant. Enraged, the Sun decided to wage a battle against Logundi.

In the battle, the Sun came down heavily upon king Logundi, burnt down all his soldiers and his family members. But Jara, who was pregnant at the time and was away at her uncle's house situated far off, was saved.

When Jara came back, she found that her father and his kingdom had been completely burnt by the Sun. As the entire kingdom was still very hot, she saved her life by throwing herself into a pot full of cool water and later escaped from the area. Eventually she bore a son and named him Jwala.

Jwala grew up into a strong, tall and dusky young boy quite resembling his mother and when he played with his teenage friends, he always stood out. His friends were jealous of him for his daredevilry. When they killed a bird or an animal, each of his friends shouted out: "I did a good thing for my father." But when Jwala killed something he always said: "I did a good thing for my mother." For a few days, the teenage boys were in utter confusion as to why Jwala kept taking his mother's name and not his father's as they did. Their curiosity grew deeper. One day, all of them surrounded Jwala and asked him, "Who is your father?"

Jwala could not say a thing as he had never thought about it earlier. But the question that his teenage friends had asked, kept ringing in his ears the whole day and when he went back home that evening, he asked his mother, "Mother, who is my father?"

Jara had tried to hide her past from her son thinking that he was still too young to take stress. But that evening, she could not control her tears and when Jwala kept looking at her eyes inquiringly, she knew she could no longer hide the truth from him. She narrated the story of how the Sun had gone crazy about her beauty and how he had desperately wanted her; and when he failed to get her, how he had wiped away all her clan in a battle against her father.

When Jara had finished the story, Jwala went to his room without saying a word, and his mother's plea to have the evening meal went off his ears. On the following day, he asked his mother to teach him his family trade of smelting iron from iron ore. The Asurs were the first people on earth to discover the knowledge of iron-smelting and Jara being the daughter of the king of Asurs, had inherited the knowledge in its fineness. She felt happy that her son had shown interest in learning the clan's knowledge.

"Before you start smelting iron, you have to offer prayers to three gods—Lohasur—the Asur god of Iron, Koylasur—the Asur god of Coal and Agneyasur—the Asur god of Fire, our family gods," said Jara to Jwala, as they went to the courtyard to set up a workshop. For each god, Jwala offered an egg for appeasement and when the workshop was ready, Jara started the lessons. She sat on a log while Jwala squatted beside her on the ground. When Jwala had understood the theoretical part of the knowledge of iron-smelting, Jara took her son to the forest to gather iron ore. She taught him how to recognise iron ore from the heaps of stones and in the evening, both of them came back with a sackful of iron ore. On the following day, the mother and son duo set off to the forest again. Jara took two dry sticks and rubbed them hard, displaying her knowledge of how to generate Virgin Fire. Jwala was a quick learner and he learnt the skill quickly from his mother. He repeated the exercise a few times and by evening, he had mastered the skill. On the third day Jara took her son again into the forest, picked up some dry *sal* logs, placed them in a pile and lit it. After some time, she asked Jwala to put out the fire by pouring water on it and thus coal was born.

The workshop of the mother and the son was successful. Had it not been for Jara who dared to teach the knowledge to her son, the discipline of iron-smelting would have died with the death of king Logundi, sacrificed to the lust of the Sun. After many weeks of long and tedious labour the first Virgin Iron, post the Sun-Logundi battle, was born.

Jwala went on smelting and making iron and his mother was happy as she gazed at his son working on his ancestors' trade. When Jwala had produced a large quantity of virgin iron, he started preparing a huge cage, weaving iron nails with one another.

"Mother," said Jwala.

"Yes Jwala, tell me," replied Jara.

"Where does the Sun live?"

"He lives thousands of miles away across seven seas and seven hills."

The following morning, Jwala got up early, went to his mother who was cooking in the kitchen and said, "Mother, give me food for twelve long years, for I will return to you only after twelve years. I am going to meet the Sun and ask him a few questions," said Jwala.

Mother understood that her son had made up his mind. She did not say a word. She served him food and herself sat beside him, looking at him as he ate. And when he had eaten his food, Jwala picked up the huge net that he had prepared out of virgin iron, looked at his mother with tears in his eyes and set off.

"Do not forget to take along with you Remi, the neighbour girl whom I know you like. I have called her here and she is standing at the door. When both of you proceed on your journey, you will come across temples of Lohasur, Koylasur and Agneyasur. Stopping at each of these temples formally tie your knots together as man and woman. My spirit will be with both of you wherever you go," said Jara.

Every evening, the Sun went to the seashore to play with his consort, the Earth and Jwala studied the timings.

The following evening, when the Sun came down to the seashore to play with the Earth, Jwala threw the net around the Sun and caged him. Jwala then tightened the iron net, and, squeezing the Sun tight into it, gathered tightly the corners of the net and tied them with a huge iron rod, leaving the Sun to agitate like a snared rabbit inside. The whole night, the Sun growled and moaned, trying to come out of the cage. Jwala stood a little away and savoured the scene, watching the enemy of his grandfather in pain. People that night waited and waited for the Sun to rise but their wait was unending. The whole world reeled under darkness and men and women started looking for the Sun, with *diya* (light) in their hands. Finally, a man managed to spot something netted inside an iron cage lying beside the seashore and groaning in pain. He went near the cage, peeped through it and saw the Sun inside it. He ran to his village to recount the scene to them. Then all the people of the world gathered beside the seashore and rescued the Sun.

'Badly bruised and tired, the Sun scrawled out of the net and when he saw Jwala walking away with Remi, now his wife, he was furious. Reeling in anger with his face red, he kicked Remi to the ground, inviting Jwala's wrath.

"You have kicked my wife instead of fighting with me. So I curse you. You will not be able to play with your consort, the Earth, any longer. When you go closer, she will be dry."

Sun's anger melted and he pleaded with Jwala to take back his curse and end the enmity. Jwala however told the

Sun that his lust had already wiped off all of the Asur clan and hence the curse shall be relaxed only a little. "Only for two months during the year, you can play with your consort, the Earth," Jwala said and then left the place with Remi.

Thus, the Sun is able to play with the Earth only for two months during the year and when he meets her, he is usually too hot. The closer he goes to his consort, the hotter he gets. After they copulate, the Earth gets pregnant and she bears offspring. Her lap gets filled with children, that is, greenery. And then men and women living on Earth's lap rejoice.

*

Surya is the blazing sun[88]. "O Surya, with the light whereby thou scatterest gloom, and with thy ray impellest every moving thing, Keep far from us all feeble, worthless sacrifice, and drive away disease and every evil dream."[89] For the Munda group also 'sun' is singi-bonga (sun spirit) and the Kherias, a tribe in the Munda group, pray to sun early in the morning thinking that the blessings of Singbonga, the Supreme Spirit is are showered on them through the rays of the sun.

Soma

Soma is the god of inspiration, the intoxicant who stirs the minds, lures the gods and brings them to the place of worship. "Thou, Soma, art pre-eminent for wisdom; along the straightest path thou art our leader. Our wise forefathers by thy guidance, Indu, dealt out among the gods their share of treasure. Thou by thine insight art most wise, O Soma, strong by thine energies and all possessing, Mighty art thou by all thy powers and greatness, by glories art thou glorious, guide of mortals."[90]

"Do thou, God Soma, with thy Godlike spirit, victorious, win for us a share of riches. Let none prevent thee: thou art Lord of valour. Provide for both sides in the fray for booty."[91]

In Munda legends, as discussed above, Mahadeo (Shiva) was the one who taught the first woman how to prepare a intoxicating drink with the use of herbs. Mundas use this drink in their rituals even to this day.

Rati or Love: The Boy and the Bird

A story is narrated by the Kherias (or Kharia), a tribe of the Munda group, at marriage ceremonies.

In a village, there lived a rich Kheria couple. After a few years, the woman bore a son, and the two started raising him with great love and care.

The child grew into an attractive young man, ever beaming with zest and joy. He loved to joke and laugh with his fellow boys and girls. One day, when the boy had become a young adult, he told his father, 'I want to go into the forest on a hunt'.

The father had not taught him how to use the bow and the arrow, how to use an axe, and how to run across huge rocks, because he did not want him to perform difficult acts. But now that the young boy had expressed his desire to go on a hunt, he had no other option but to initiate him into using a bow and the art of hunting and other acts of courage.

First he taught him how to use the bow and arrow. Then he taught him how to use the axe.

Within a few days the boy mastered the art of using a bow, and then displayed equal mastery over the use of the axe. He could shoot down the flying birds and fell them; he could run up to a hill with speed and climb down with equal lightning swiftness. The father presented him with his own bow and arrows that he had inherited from his own father and preserved as a prized possession. He also presented him with a sharp axe.

'Carry enough cool water in a tumba and go,' said his father, wishing his son good luck on his first ever hunting expedition. *Tumba* is a water-container made of dry pumpkin.

He carried the bow and arrows on his shoulders, took the axe in one hand and proceeded into the deep forest. He roamed around the forest looking for deer, wild boar and rabbits. But to his bad luck, he found none.

After some time, he came to a tree and lay down under its cool little shade to relax. The tree was tall. After a while, a sweet feeble voice reached his ears. The voice slowly grew louder. And the louder it grew the sweeter it sounded. Curious, the boy looked up, but saw nothing. He tried to listen to it intently, straining his ears a bit.

'It is a baby bird singing sweetly,' he said to himself and got up.

The boy tried to spot the baby bird now. He looked for it on the branches of the tree, but could not find it anywhere. He wondered where the baby bird perched and sweet-sounded him.

The boy now listened more intently. He realised that the voice came from the trunk of a tree.

'The baby bird must be up there but how do I get there? I will have to climb the tree,' he thought.

The tree was slim. His father had not taught him how to climb trees. And this tree had no branches to hold on to!

'I will crawl up the tree,' the boy thought.

He embraced the tree with all his might and crawled up. And while doing so he felt a pleasant sensation. But after reaching a point, he felt tired, and was unable to move further.

'What do I do now?' the boy asked himself.

He remained at the spot, embracing the tree for some time. But his heart kept saying that he should move up to reach the point from where the sweet voice came. He tried to see that point—it was just above.

The boy raised his eyes. 'Wow, I have something to hold on to in order to move upwards.'

The boy had spotted two rounded protrusions that were jutting out of the tree. The boy slowly moved his hand to one of them and caught one of them.

Again, he felt nice and the baby bird started to sing even more sweetly. He put his other hand on the second rounded mass. The baby bird now burst forth with cries of divine joy, sounds that he had never heard in the forest before. The boy too felt a heavenly rapture, something he had never experienced before. He stayed there in a state of bliss.

'Don't waste your time staying there. Look here...' the boy heard a voice from below.

The boy looked down and saw that there was small hole below the rounded mass.

'The baby bird is inside. It is singing sweetly from this tiny hole,' the boy told himself.

The boy did not want to leave the rounded mass. But the voice cried again: "Will you not take me home? I am here.'

He looked down, then slowly took one hand off the rounded mass and placed it in the tiny hole. It was very smooth. He found that the baby bird was in divine ecstasy.

The boy had now grown into an adult, ready to play another role in life.

*

Rati is the Hindu goddess of love, carnal desire, lust, passion and sexual pleasure. She is the female counterpart, the chief consort and the assistant of Kama (Kamadeva), the god of love. Rishi Agastya's wife Lopamudra invites goddess Rati and Kamadeva to energise her husband to make love to her.[92] A constant companion of Kama, she is often depicted with him in legend and temple sculpture. She also enjoys worship along with Kama. Rati is often associated with the arousal and delight of sexual activity, and many sex techniques and positions derive their Sanskrit names from hers. The Hindu scriptures stress Rati's beauty and sensuality.

Agni

The very first poem of the Rigveda (Rigveda 1.1) invokes Agni: 'Agni who is common to all men'. It starts as: 'I praise Agni, minister and divine priest of the ritual, who as invoker brings most treasure'.

On the other hand in Munda tradition, the Fire deity *Agni* is known as *Agneyasur* (the Fire deity), as called by the Agarias, a branch of the Munda group of tribes. In fact, Verrier Elwin in his book *Agaria*, talks of deities like Lohasur (the deity of iron) and Koylasur (the deity of coal). Asur-Agarias being an artisans group who used to be very powerful during the formation of *junapadas* (tribal confederations) due to their knowledge of iron-smelting, had to worship Agneyasur, Lohasur and Koylasur—three important deities, if they wanted to smelt iron, out of which weapons were made for wars. Arrival of iron in India is credited to Asur-Agarias[93]. Elwin in his book narrates a legend in which how Nanga Baiga, in order to prepare an iron nail, broke a huge stone with his hand. In the process, there appeared iron (later worshipped as *Lohasur*) and spark of fire (worshipped as Agneyasur)[94]. There is a belief among the people of Munda tribes that if someone pisses on fire, his penis will swell and develop wound. Any kind of disrespect to fire in any form is prohibited among the Mundas. 'Wearing red clothes and entering an iron-smelting worskshop is strictly prohibited among Agarias. An incident took place in a village near Karanjia when a youth named Chandiya Agaria entered a workshop wearing red clothes and caught fire. There is another reason to this prohibition: the offering made to Agneyasur has to be usually a red cock'[95].

*

Atharvaveda

This story is narrated by P.P. Hembrom, a learnt and famous ethno-botanist of Jharkhand, who figures in Who's Who of '*A-Z in Ethnobotany,'96* authored by S.K. Jain and Ashok K. Jain. S.K. Jain is also known as the Father of Ethnobotany in India, and Hembrom, who was a forest officer trained before Indepedence, was often consulted by Jain. The story is about the origin of Ethno-medicine:

"There lived a tribal chieftain named Dhantari. He was born with immense innate knowledge of herbs and their use as medicine in different diseases. His reputation grew far and wide and hundreds of sick men and women would visit him every day to seek medical advice and treatment. Dhantari treated them with love and care using the herbs he knew, which were aplenty all around the forest that lay beyond his fort.

In the country lived the witches too, who practised out black magic on individuals they did not like. Black magic was also practised by the witches upon innocent individuals just for the fun of it. However, the victims would walk miles to visit Dhantari to seek treatment. Dhantari knew which disease was caused due to anomaly in the body and which was caused due to black magic. He would reveal the fact to the victims. While the popularity of Dhantari kept growing every day, the witches became more and more unpopular and were despised by men and women alike in the whole country.

With number of patients growing every day, Dhantari all alone could no longer treat all the sick people seeking medicine and advice. He decided to make a few disciples and with that intention set up a school. He would take his students to the forest and educate them on how to recognise trees, herbs, plants and grass; and their use for different diseases. Days passed and nights were spent in grinding herbs to prepare medicine. The witches, meanwhile, got alarmed. 'If Dhantari manages to pass on all his knowledge to his students before he dies, we will be of no use. All our black magic will be of no use. People, who fear us now, will no longer fear us. We must do something'—they thought.

One night the witches gathered to discuss what they must do. One of them mooted the idea that they must cast a spell on Dhantari himself. Initially, they wanted to desist from doing so, but slowly the evil thought got hold of them. One night, the spell was cast on Dhantari and the master healer himself fell seriously ill.

The following morning when the disciples gathered in the school they found their master seriously ill. They tried to diagnose the illness, but could not fathom what it was and how it could be treated. The disciples did not know the medicine for the illness Dhantari had. Meanwhile, the condition of Dhantari was becoming worse as hours passed.

He called all his disciples to himself and told them: 'Look I am very sick. Unfortunately, I am yet to teach you the medicine for the disease that I have. I am not able to walk and hence I cannot go to the place where the herbs to treat this disease are located. But two of you must proceed to the south, cross two hills and arrive in a ravine. You will find a few huge *saal* (shorea robusta) trees. Beside them, you will come across a few climbers with palm-like leaves. Dig the climbers and get some roots,' Dhantari commanded.

Two disciples set out to the south into deep forest as their master Dhantari had directed. They crossed the first hill and when they were passing by the second, they came across a few women who were picking leaves from the trees. Though the women, who actually were witches, knew that the two young men were disciples of Dhantari, they asked them who they were and where they were going. The young men were simple-hearted without jealousy and evil, and hence they told them what they were up to. 'Your master has cheated you. He does not want you to know where the real medicine is. We have just seen such herbs in the far west as we were coming. So go to the west. Hurry!'

Back in the fort, Dhantari waited for his disciples to come with the medicine. But when he saw that they were making undue delay, he understood that they must have gone astray. He then called two other young men and with similar instruction sent them to fetch the herbs. On the way they were met by the same witches, and the witches misled them too. Dhantari sent another group, but the witches did the same with them too. A few disciples remained with Dhantari and those who went out looking for medicine, were still to return. When Dhantari realised that he was not going to survive, he told his disciples: 'If I die, do not bury my body as you do with the other dead. Cut my body into pieces and eat the pieces. This is the only way you will collectively learn all the herbal knowledge that I have in me. If you do not eat my body, all my knowledge will go with me for ever'. Saying this, Dhantari breathed his last.

When the disciples were on their way back, the witches met them again and poisoned their mind further. 'We have heard that your master has asked the disciples to eat pieces of his dead body. What kind of a master he is? Never do that'. When they returned, disciples found the other disciples urging them to take home pieces of the dead body of their master and they recalled what the witches had said. They fought with the disciples who had urged them to eat pieces of the master's dead body. However, when insisted on the orders of the master they took the pieces of flesh and bones along but threw them on the way. Pieces of Dhantari's dead body fell in the rivulets, forests and open fields. Only those disciples whom the master had conversed with and commanded them to eat his body parts, did so. Soon after they ate, they started feeling that knowledge of their master had been transferred to them. But it was only some portion of the knowledge, and not the complete knowledge. Disciples, who did not eat the parts of the body, did not get any knowledge.

Meanwhile, animals and birds picked up from the ground the body parts of Dhantari and ate from them. They inherited the herbal knowledge that Dhantari had. This is why animals and birds have natural instincts for herbal medicine, and humans have to observe them and learn from them. Some disciples inherited Dhantari's herbal knowledge, but the complete herbal knowledge got distributed among humans, animals and birds—collectively inherited from the master healer."

*

The legend is not widely known even among the tribes. With the arrival of allopathy and its popularisation as modern education spread among the Mundas, knowledge of herbal medicine has enormously dwindled in the tribal communities. It may be just a legend, but existence of a place in the state of Chhattisgarh in Central India with the name 'Dhamtari', probably named after the legendary Dhantari, makes it more than just a legend.

Ayurveda talks of Dhanvantari as the originator of herbal medicinal knowledge. It considers Dhanvantari as the god of Ayurveda medicine and an 'avatara' of Lord Vishnu. He is supposed to have arisen during the *samudramanthan* from the 'ocean of milk', according to Ayurveda.

Ayurveda is drawn from the Atharvaveda. "It is less similar to the Rigveda. The composer-priests were Angiras and Bhargavas, sometimes excluded from the 'Three Vedas' into which they were officially incporporated when the 'Four Vedas' were established"[97]. The Atharvaveda consists chiefly of "sorcery invocations (black and white magic), speculative or mystery poetry, fragments of *grihya* 'domestic' and royal rituals, as well as more specific compositions such as those that are linked to the arts of healing"[98]. Things like sorcery abound in Munda tradition, which has complicated belief in witchcraft—witchcraft is not found in the Rigveda. The very subject of sorcery seems to arise only when one believes in the Asur-women-turned *bongas* (spirits), who, it is believed, have the power to cause illness.

'If broken, if inflamed is your own bone, your flesh, Dhaatar shall fix it whole, he shall put together joint with joint' (Paippalapada Samhita 4:15). This hymn talks of '*Dhaatar*, the arranger, the creator"[99]. A different hymn (Paippalapada Smhita 6:14) talks of 'various noxious creatures'[100]: 'The knee-hairy Asurian demon that roams here, that seeks out the absent-minded one; the Arayas that are…. that are…, and on the hair, the ones that are *Svakiskin*: these do we cause to vanish from here. The Asurian friend who eats a man's young boys, the hairy, dreadful Araya who slays and eats men: him do we cause to vanish from here'[101].

The *Bhavprakash Nighantu, The Indian Materia Medica of Shri Bhava Mishra,* jointly authored by professors of Ayurvedic Science at Banaras Hindu University, Gangasahay Pandey and Krishnachandra Chunekar, too says that Ayurveda is incomplete and further information on herbs and their medicinal usage should be collected and documented from amirs, kols, kirats and hunters—in other words from tribes[102]. According to P.P. Hembrom, Mundas and other tribes across India have collective knowledge of around 4,000 herbs and plants, and their medicinal use while Aryurveda is so far able to deal with only 400 herbs and plants.

Nature Gods

The first Indo-Aryans, inhabiting by the Great Mountain Range of the North, bound as they were to be awe-inspired by the mammoth power of Nature, took this as 'god', and attributed personal characteristics to it. The personified forces of nature changed into gods and these later became one personal and transcendental God, the 'Custodian of the Cosmic Moral Order', who Himself later on passed into the immanent Purusha. The Upanishads developed this Purusha into Brahman or Atman which is both immanent and tracsendent.

Going by the Purushasukta, at times it seems that there evolved the concept of monotheism and later this monotheism branched out into polytheism. But at other times, one feels that polytheism came first and then later philosophical deliberations led to monotheism in Aryan religious development. However, it will always remain a difficult question to answer.

The Rigveda, Hymn X, 129—Hymn of Creation, (Translation by A.A. Macdonnel, and quoted by by Swami Nikhilananda in his book *"The Upanishad"* p. 19), says:

'Non-being then existed not nor being:
There was no air, no sky that is beyond it.
What was concealed? Wherein? In whose protection?
And was there deep unfathomable water?

Death then existed not nor life immortal;
Of neither night nor day was any token.
By its inheritance force of the One breathed breathless:
No other thing than that beyond existed.

Darkess there was at first by darkness hidden;
Without distinctive marks, this all was water.
That which, becoming, by the void was covered,
That One by force of heat came into being.

Desired entered the One in the beginning:
It was the earliest seed, of thought the product.
The sages searching in their hearts with wisdom,
Found out the bond of being in non-being.

Their ray extended light across the darkness:
But was the One above or was it under?
Creative force was there, and fertile power:
Below was energy, above was impulse.

Who knows for certain? Who shall here declare it?
Whence was it born, and whence came this creation?
The gods were born after this world's creation:
Then who came to know from whence it has arisen?

None knoweth whence creation has arisen;
And whether he has or he has not produced it:
He who surveys it in the highest heaven,
He only knows, or haply he may know not."

This poem, according to Vedic scholar Frits Staal, belongs to the late Rigveda when the Veda reflected a great variety of ideas, cultures and sections of society. Staal himself, however, like the following translation of the HYMN OF CREATION, as done in 1999 by Joel Brereton, claiming it to be the most recent and reliable:

1. The non-existent did not exist, nor did the existent, exist at that time.There existed neither the midspace nor heaven beyond.

   What stirred? From where and in whose protection?

   Did water exist, a deep depth?

2. Death did not exist nor deathlessness then.

   There existed no sign of night nor day.

   That one breathed without wind through its inherent force.

   There existed nothing else beyond that.

3. Darkness existed, hidden by darkness, in the beginning

   All this was a signless ocean.

   When the thing coming into being was concealed

   by emptiness, then was the One born by the power of heat.

4. Then, in the beginning, from thought developed desire,

   Which existed as the primal semen.

   Searching in their hearts through inspired thinking,

   Poets found the connection of the existence in the non-existent.

5. Their cord was stretched across:

   Did something below it? Did something exist above?

   There were places of semen and there were powers.

   There was inherent force below, offering above.

6. Who really knows? Who shall here proclaim it?

   From there was it born, from where this creation?

   The gods are on this side of this world.

   So then who does know from where it came to be?

7. This creation—from where it came to be,

   If it was produced or if not—

   He who is the overseer of this world in the highest heaven,

   He surely knows. Or if he does not know...?

"This poem recognises a genuine problem of philosophy at a level most religious poetry does not even touch. Since it can speak for itself and speaks well, I need only add that translation can do full justice to the sounds of the original,"[103] is how Staal comments on the translation of the orginal Sanksrit verses.

On the other hand, HYMN TO PRAJAPATI (Rig Veda X, Hymn 121, *translated by R.T.H. Griffith*) goes thus:

'In the beginning rose Hiranyagarbha, born only lord of all created beings.

He fixed and holdeth up this earth and heaven. What god shall we adore with our oblations?

Giver of vital breath, of power and vigour, he whose commandments all the gods acknowledge:

Whose shade is death, whose lustre makes immortal. What god shall we adore with our oblation?

Who by the grandeur has become the sole ruler of all moving world that breathes and slumber;

He who is lord of men and lord of cattle. What god shall we adore with our oblarion?

His, through high might, are these snow-capped mountains, and men call sea and Raja his possession:

His arms are these, his are these heavenly regions. What god shall we adore with our oblation?

By him the heavens are strong and earth steadfast, by him lights realm and sky-vault are supported:

By him the regions in mid-air measured. What god shall we adore with our oblation?

To him, supported by his help, two armies look while trembling in their spirit,'

When over them the risen sun is shining. What god shall we adore with our oblation?

What time the mighty waters came, containing the universal gems, producing Agni,

Hence sprang the gods' spirit into being. What god shall we adore with our oblation?

He in his might surveyed the floods containing productive force and generating worship.

He is the god of gods, and none beside him. What god shall we adore with our oblation?

Ne'er ay he harm us who is earth's begetter, nor he whose laws are sure the heavens' creator,

He who brought forth the great and lucid waters. What god shall we adore with our oblation?'

*

Interestingly, both the Hymns point to monotheism to be existing in the beginning among the Indo-Aryans. However, the reality of belief in many gods (polytheism), as enumerated before, belief in different gods, cannot be overlooked.

'If there is polytheism in the Vedas, then how is it that the binding principle of this world, the Supreme Soul of this Universe, the Guardian of this Cosmos, is so much emphasised and repeated?'[104]

Again when polytheism leads to monotheism, the most powerful among the hierarchy of gods is enthroned as the ruler of this universe. But this is conspicuous by its absence in the Vedas—gods were regarded as the manifestation of one Supreme God, so that any god who was worshipped, ultimately the Supreme God was worshipped. The Vedas stands for the purest type of monotheism:

'Ekam sad vipra bahudha vedanti'[105]: *The One Real, the wise declare as many.*

"The gods are praised, yet not gods but God is praised through them. Hence there is no development through polytheism to monotheism and monisim, but only of monism from the first Mantra portion of the last Upanishadic portion."[106]

On the other hand, the extreme orthodox views that Vedas are authorless and eternal, too, cannot be philosophically sustained. "The correct position seems to be that the Vedic sages were intensely intellectual and immensely spiritual and this mystic experience, this direct intutitive spiritual insight overflew into literature as the Vedic hymns.'[107]

Even Staal refutes the orthodox view of authorlessness of the Vedas. "It nowhere says that the Veda is *revealed* or *sruti*, literally 'what is heard'. It is heard in the sense that it is transmitted from father to son or from teacher to pupil. The Vedas are an Oral Tradition and that applies especially to two of the four: Veda of the Verse (*Rig-veda*) and the Veda of the Chants (*Sama-veda*).... These poets were not addressed by gods. They used brahman of Vedic invocations to *address* gods. I have translated brahman as 'language' and not 'speech'."[108]

God is the Ultimate Reality (Brahman), and the word finds mention in the Veda ample number of times. The word is derived from the root *'brh'* which means *to grow or to evolve*. "In the beginning it meant sacrifice, then prayer and then it acquired its present meaning of ultimate reality which evolves itself as this world."[109]

Vedic philosophers, especially Sankara, Ramanuja and Madhava have discourced at length while dealing with relations of *Brahman* and *Creation*, and have evolved philosophical traditions famously known as *Advaita* (Non-Dualism), *Visisthadvaita* (Qualified Non-Dualism) and Dvaita (Dualism) respecitively, dwelling upon the Upanishads. Further, the Upanishads describe the *Brahman* both with *attributes (Saguna Brahman)* and *without attributes (Nirguna Brahman)*.

Ultimate Reality, according to Sankara, is *Brahman* or *Atman*, which is *Pure Consciousness, devoid of all attributes (nirguna)*. Brahman associated with its *potency (shakti) maya* appears as the *qualified Brahman (saguna)* or Iswra, who is Creator, Preserver and Destroyer of this world which is His Appearance.

On the other hand, Ramanuja attempts a harmonious combination of absolutism with personal theism. The Absolute, according to Ramanuja, is an organic unity (visishtha), an identity which is qualified by diversity (vishesanas).[110]

Ramanuja admits the reality of this world too and says that 'God is also the soul of souls. Our souls are souls in relation to our bodies, but in relation to God, they become His body and He is their soul.'[111]

Madhava, meanwhile, is the sworn critic of Sankara and his *Advaitavad* (Non-Dualism) and like Ramanuja, he believes in God, soul and matter (Creation) as three entities which are eternal and absolutely real, though soul and matter are dependent on God. God alone is independent. "He [God] has a divine body and is transcendent. But He is also immanent as the inner ruler of all souls. He damns some and redeems others. He is a perfect personality."[112] Madhava is a ranked dualist and does not believe in qualified absolutism.[113]

❑

CHAPTER 5

Man, Woman: Heart and Soul

The nature of a man or woman is similar to the nature of the Divinity or she worships. In order to understand a person, one has to understand the kind of God the said person believes in. Critical analysis of the Legend of Creation, and Asur Legend, Legend of Procreation will suggest that an individual with the background of these legends will invariably be a Munda in nature and culture. Man is the highest creature of animate and inanimate beings that Singbonga created. He created Man-Woman with intelligence, someone who can understand Singbonga more than others do, with whom Singbinga can relate.

Man is not the *Master* of Creation, as in the Bible—where the entire Creation is placed before Man to rule over. Since

Man has intelligence, he has to be Singbonga-like in nature, and Singbonga is all caring and providing, Man has to be caring and providing towards all. In other sense, Man has to play as the caretaker of all the beings in creation, not its destroyer. The moment he tries to destroy or become a threat to the existence of any of the created beings, Singbonga will bring about his destruction. Or destruction will naturally follow—just as it happened in the Asur Legend. Man has to play his role as Caretaker of Creation, and not as Master of Creation. Only the Singbonga is the Master and none else.

If Man has to work only to fulfil his greed the whole day and night, this will only bring destruction as Asur Legend reveals. Man has to work during the day and rest during the night—soon after night falls. Songs and dances have been created for man in order to relax.

Man and Woman are created at the same time, from the same stuff (born from eggs simultaneously), unlike in Christianity where the Woman is created out of the bones of Man, after the Man. In the *Sirjan Kani*, Singbonga made the idols of Man and Woman simultaneously at the same time, and not one after the other (Man and then the Woman). This is why gender equality is the norm in the social structure of Munda tribes, coming down straight from the Legend of Creation.

Doing anti-social work is sin, and living in the society is sacred. Man has to observe festivals—set by Singbonga and specially remember Him, recalling the Creation: Mage, Ba (Sarhul) being the most important of festivals when Singbonga specially comes and rests on *Shorea robusta* (sal tree).

Since Singbonga comes and rests in *Shorea robusta*, and since the Asur women's spirits rest on different things and take care of them on the order of the Singbonga, Man should not destroy anything of the Creation. For, this will bring about destruction of the Earth. Destruction of the Earth will bring about the destruction of human beings.

A Munda man has to have a Woman and live with her, because it is not good for him to live alone. They should have sex and procreation.

Man necessarily is 'good' but his greed for riches and power may make him evil as indicated in the Asur Legend. And when this happens, Man fails to see reason to correct himself, because he becomes blind in his greed for riches and power. In the Asur Legend, Singbonga sends many messengers for the Asurs, but they fail to convince them. Instead, they are chased away after being insulted. Man does not want to sacrifice his own progeny, but he is ever willing to find a victim in other community for the sacrifice. Thus, man knows that sacrificing to God or deity—particularly when it comes to human sacrifice is 'bad' as long as the victim is one of his kin, and when the victim could be anybody, even outside the clan, then even this 'bad' becomes 'not objected'. Thus, Man's rationality does not always decide what is 'good' and what is 'bad'—this issue is decided by who is involved—my own kin or someone else, as derived from the Asur Legend.

Soul

Soul is that which survives the body after the death of a person, and is called 'ji' (Hasda Mundari dialect) or 'jiu' (in

Naguri Mundari). Though Mundas are unhesitating and staunch believers in the soul as distinct from the body and as surviving later, they distinguish in its various functions. They also use a term 'roa', which in itself is not *ji* (soul). They use another term—*Umbul* (shade), which too, in itself is not *ji* (soul). But collectively, the two: *Roa* and *Umbul*, form the *Ji* (soul), as one complete entity. But this is only when the person in whom *Roa* and *Umbil* both rest as *Ji*, is alive. When the person dies, *Roa* gets separated from *Umbul* and can either move to *sirma* (heaven) or take rebirth. The *Umbul* does not move to *sirma*, neither does it take rebirth. If the person dying lived a noble life, the *Umbul* is welcomed back into the house and given a corner to reside. The *Umbul* of the dead ancestor lives in the house itself and protects the members every minute.

The *ji* (soul) is considered the Efficient Cause of all the processes of the bodily life. It is therefore said to be present everywhere in the whole body and acts. During dream it is *roa*, not the *umbul* in the *ji*, which leaves the body and wanders about: it is not good to wake people abruptly without leaving the *roa* time to re-enter the body.[114]

After the death of a person, when the *'umbul'* has been recalled to the house, it is called *'orah-bonga'* (house spirit). Mundas hold an elaborate function to recall the *umbul* of a person after his death.

Ji (soul), further, is the principle of life found not only in men, but also in animals and plants. In plants, however, it has only the vegetative power, in animals moreover it has faculty of sensuous perception and the appetitive and locomotive faculties; in man, in addition to all these, it has reason and rational appetitive or will. The ji as endowed with reason and will, has also *mon* (mind).

When a plant or animal dies, its ji dwindles into the air, i.e.; it disappears, it is annihilated. The ji of a man is immortal and, when he dies, goes to the '*bitarpur*'[115], the inner dwelling, also called '*porom disom*'[116], the country beyond (the next world) there to receive from Singbonga a reward or punishment.

"The roa on the contrary is not bound to remain continually in the body during life. As a matter of fact, nearly every night when the body lies down to sleep and the *umbul* has to remain there, the *roa* is off for an outing. *Roa* sees and hears when it thus wanders about. Nevertheless, it should not remain absent for too long. A few hours can do no harm, but if it remains weeks or months without returning, the body is affected by a chronic disease and is on the way to death"[117].

The Mundas have a whole theory of genesis and interpretation of dreams. *Roa* is indeed of a moving nature: nearly every night, while the body sleeps, it is off for an outing. What we call dreams is just what our *roa* sees and hears on these trips.

"Often, if not always, *roa* then sees things not as actually they are in progress but as they are going to happen shortly. When free of the body it is gifted with a prophetic insight into the near future. It may moreover either see the actors of these events in their unveiled reality, just as they are or it may see then under symbolic appearance. The latter is the usual way: an individual man is nearly always seen by the wandering *roa* under the shape of such animal as he resembles by character or, at least, a man stands for an animal, and vice versa. Thus, if in a dream one sees a person dying, it means that either he is going to kill some game in the chase of that he is going to lose one of his domestic animals. If he dreams of a dying animal, he must expect the demise of a member of his own household, a co-villager or other relation. If he dreams that an animal enters his house, he knows that he will soon have a visitor or guest. If he meets a man in his dream, he will in reality come across an animal. A snake indicates a quiet but successful man, an elephant a quiet but fearless one".[118]

Interestingly, the Munda theory of soul manages to satisfactorily explain why man remains alive when he sleeps like the dead, with his soul out sojourn in dream, encountering other souls alike.

The *umbul* (shade) on the other hand, is the part of the soul which remains forever in the house of his descendants after the death of the physical body, and the Mundas have a ceremony to invite the umbul back into the house. *Umbul* (shade) is not the soul, but the outer part that the *roa* parts with when ji leaves the body. The *roa* of the person who lives a good life, leaves for *sirma* (heaven) to live with Singbonga, while his *umbul* remains with the family after the death of the person. The family members assign a corner of the house for this umbul, where the *umbul* (shade) of the person lives and protects the members from all evil.

On the other hand, if the person has not been able to live a noble life, his *roa* may take a rebirth (get embodied) and in the process acquire a new *umbul.* The *roa* usually takes rebirth in the family itself or in the same clan, as human being. If a child is born soon after the death of an elderly person, the child would get the name of the elderly person. It is believed that the grandfather's soul is again born in the same house as the grandson[119]. However, the new child's body acquires a new *umbul* (shade), and the *umbul* of the grandfather would be assigned a corner to live by.

The roa of the dead does not enter a non-human body to take rebirth; whenever it takes a rebirth, it is always as human being. Noble living, according to Munda worldview, is living an upright and moral life, prescribed by the Munda society, a harmonious and loving life with other people in the society, without hatred, jealousy, greed or ill-will.

Thus, the concept of *karma*, as defined in the Vedas, is partially found in the Munda philosophy. On the other hand, there is a belief that if someone is evil by action, he is punished by Singbonga and he usually meets an unnatural death, and his *ji* keeps wandering about all through. His *umbul* (shade) too is not invited back into the house. There is no *rebirth* for such 'soul' and the soul becomes an evil spirit.

Sex

In the Munda Legend of Creation, Singbonga created Man and Woman as a pair and let them live together. Singbonga wanted the human couple to copulate and multiply, but as they lived like brother and sister, He Himself had to come and initiate them into sex, after formally performing a marriage ceremony in his own way.

Thus, Mundas do look upon man's living with woman as necessary and natural, and living single as against the decree of Singbonga. Sex is looked upon as natural, but only with the spouse and no other person. Sex outside marriage in a situation when the spouse is active in all respect is looked down upon. In case of inactiveness of the spouse, however, second wife is allowed for the man; and for the woman too, she can always leave him and find a virile man to live with.

Sex before marriage, however, is an alien concept in Munda community though it has arrived in the new age with social change, just as it has done in other communities and traditions. Munda boys and girls grow together side by side without even a trace of thought of having sex with each other. In recent days, however, modern education and influence of modernisation has been promoting sporadic instances of premarital sex between Munda boys and girls.

Nature: Are Mundas Nature Worshippers?

Creation (Nature) holds a very significant place in the Munda worldview and philosophy. Going by the Legend of Creation, Singbonga appears to have created the Earth, and thereupon the Nature, animals and birds, before He created the Man and the Woman, so that when the two come into being, they have a ready dwelling place and food. Among all the other creatures of Creation, Singbonga created Man as the most intelligent, compassionate, rational and thinking creature. However, he did not make Man the master of the Creation, did not place the Creation at his feet to do whatever he liked to do with it. He gave the Creation to Man to live in, assigned him a place whereby, being superior among other creatures in the Creation, he should take care of them and keep them secure, healthy and happy. That is why when the Asurs started over-exploiting the Nature for their greed and pride, Singbonga decided to set things in order. The grass, the trees and the herbs were withering due to excessive heat of the furnace of the Asurs where they smelted iron day in and day out, in order to get richer and more powerful. The animals did not get water, because even the water sources were drying up; men did not get food and water because the fruit-bearing trees had been negatively affected by the environmental hazard caused by excessive heat. Singbonga then decided to send a message to the Asurs thrice to amend their ways. But when the Asurs did not relent in their evil ways, Singbonga decided to come down Himself and destroy them.

Thus, Munda people draw lessons from the Asur Legend and play their role to safeguard and protect the Nature, just as they may use it for their sustenance. Over the centuries, a symbiotic relationship has emerged between the Mundas and Nature. A Munda cannot imagine his life without Nature, and Nature's existence without the care and protection of the Munda cannot be imagined.

Further in the same Asur Legend, Singbonga dropped the women of the Asur men who had caught hold of His different parts as He rose up to *Sirma* (Heaven), and they fell on different places. Some fell on the rivulets, some on the fields, some on the pebbles, some on the trees, some on the hills, some on the paddy fields, some in the village, and the like. Singbonga ordered them to take care of the places where they fell and in return, they would get food and water from the people. These Asur women became spirits (*bongas*) and took care of the places where they fell. And, the people keep making offering of food and water to these spirits (*bongas*). When the Mundas offer food and water to the bongas, only after invoking the name of Singbonga, the act appears as if they are worshipping Nature. In fact, the Munda belief goes that Singbonga comes down to the Earth and resides in Nature, particularly in Saal tree (*Shorea robusta*). And hence the usual practice is that the Munda *pahan* sets up his worshipping place near a Saal tree and performs the worship for Singbonga. He may likewise set up his his place of worship in hills and rivulets where Singbonga can come down and reside as he pleases. Thus, the practice may not actually be called Nature worship per se, but worshipping near the Nature is what is required to worship Singbonga. In a situation where the *pahan* cannot set up his place of worship near a tree, he may cut a branch of the tree and plant it in his courtyard beside which he will set up his worshipping place to worship Singbonga. This is particularly true during Sarhul festival, the festival of flowers usually observed in the Spring Season when Saal tree starts flowering. Singbonga, thus, identifies himself with Nature by His very Omnipotence and Omnipresence—which is how Nature worship of the Mundas is viewed. Nature is not Singbonga but Singbonga is in Nature. Singbonga has necessarily to be worshipped under the vast open sky, in Nature. He cannot be worshipped in a building, like the temple or church, for He cannot reside or rest anywhere else other than in Nature.

And the common belief propagated by scholars (lacking indepth knowledge of the Munda religious belief system and limited only to books) that Singbonga is 'Sun God' (*Spirit of Light)* and hence even Sun is worshipped as Singbonga, is vehemently denied by the Mundas. Singbonga being Omnipotent and Omnipresent may choose to live in the Sun, which has been created by Him, as per the belief of the Mundas. But, the Sun itself, is not Singbonga, neither do the Mundas believe that He lives in the Sun. The 'Sun' in Mundari is called *'singi'* and not *'sing'* (supreme), Singbonga should not be confused with *Singi-bonga*—a word which is not only meaningless to them but also does not exist in Munda lexicon. On the other hand, the Kherias, a kin of the Munda tribe, who also form part of the larger Munda Tribes, see the blessings of the Supreme Spirit coming through the rays of the sun. They believe that their Supreme God, Ponomoshor, cannot be seen but as He is powerful as the Sun, he can be felt coming to meet them every time the Sun rays reach them. And this is why they rever the Sun (Bero). In fact, their day begins with reverence to the Sun, by facing east with folded hands. By doing this they however symbolically believe that they worship their Ponomoshor—who is the most powerful supernatural being.

SANTALS

The Santal's concept of Man is as much interesting. The concept of Santal Man has to be drawn from the Santal Story of Creation.

A Santal is a man close to God—who is supposed to spend his entire life in His care and guidance, and any big step he takes only after getting assured that the work is an 'order' from this Thakur—just as it happened in the case of Santal Hul. It happens because of Santal man's close association with his Creator God. Santal's God is a 'Relational God', and hence Santals have to be 'relational being'—in the sense that they have to relate to each other and live. In fact, a true Santal cannot live without talking, Santal men and women have to be a talkative lot. In real life too, Santals are real *chatter boxes*—usually when they are among themselves.

Man is basically a religious being, from birth till death and after. All the decisions and actions of a Santal have to be in keeping with the purpose of the Creator God, Thakur jiu. Man is essentially innocent. In the Santal Legend of Creation, the Evil Spirit corrupts with intoxicant 'pride and covetousness'. Man is essentially a moral being. A Santal's length and breadth of moral code and conduct has its origin in living as a community, divided into different clans (totems), the whole community has a set of moral code and conduct wherein each clan has its own. Insulting the community is the biggest sin; not going by the collective decision of the community is the biggest evil. Therefore, Santal man has little scope for independent personal thought on traditional and community subjects.

Soul

The Santals believe that the present life does not end with death. What a Santal believes is that both the present state of life and the state of life after death is in the hands of God. Therefore, Santal's religious concern begins right from his birth. The word for 'soul' is *'jivi'*, which is immortal and part of God[120]. It is the living force in human life, which makes human beings capable of acting, reasoning and moving.

"The Santals have a strong belief in life in this world and its continuation in the next world. Thus the Santals take this present life seriously because the future would be determined on the basis of the present life in this world. Life in this world is as much important as the life in the next world. So they believe in the immortality of the soul".[121]

Kheria

Philosophical concept of Man in the Kherias has to be drawn up mostly from the Legend of Creation and Legend of Procreation that the tribesmen never tire of narrating at every public function. Man is created by a Supreme Being. The Earth is created by the same Supreme Being especially for Man, which will offer him a suitable dwelling place, food and water. Trees and plants have been created for his sustenance.

The main task of the Man is to praise Ponomoshor and offer regular sacrifice to Him, remembering His power, splendour and generosity. Man is normally good, but greed, selfishness and pride may make him evil and bring about his destruction. There is gender equality, and Man is not superior to Woman. In fact, when it comes to making big decision, woman may take the initiative just as Dakai Rani refused to hand over the boy and the girl—Jerka and Jerki, to Ponomoshor; and in the process, Ponomoshor had to make the promise to her, and not to Sembhu. This gender equality also is derived from the fact that Man and Woman came into life simultaneously, and not that Man came to life first and then the Woman—as in case of Christianity

(Abrahamic tradition). This gender equality and women often taking lead in many matters can, in real situation, be found in the Kherias.

Life After Death and Rebirth

Kherias partially believe in the 'Life after Death' concept. Man, according to the Legend of Creation, is made of two parts: Body and Soul—while Dakai Rani has the right over human Body, Ponomoshor has the right over Human Soul. "Kherias believe in the rebirth. But while the concept of rebirth in Hinduism is based on *Karma* and it is according to one's *Karma* that he is born out of different kinds of 'yoni', Kherias do not have the concept of *Karma*. They believe that a Kheria is re-born as a *Kheria* again after his death in some other family. Thus, the older generation always remains in the community in the form of younger generation, but after the death of the person, he forgets everything that he went through in the first life and begins his next life all over again, in the next birth"[122].

Soul (Jiyom) and Shade (Longoy)

Kherias conceive that a man has two essential things in his body, apart from his physical body: *jiyom* (soul) and *longoy* (shade). *Jiyom* is the 'Life Breath' which comes from Ponomoshor himself, and 'longoy' is the shade that his physical body produces. While the soul cannot die and cannot be destroyed—just as in other traditions, this *longoy* in Kharia tradition continues to exist even after the death of a person, just as it did when the person was alive. While the *jiyom* (soul) gets rebirth, the *longoy* (shade) of a dead person (or ancestor) is taken back through a ceremony into the house and given a resting place—usually in a corner of the kitchen. This *Longoy* (shade) of the ancestor continues to live in the house of the person's descendants while *jiyom* (soul) may take a rebirth again, as a Kheria in any part of the world. Even the *Longoy* is indestructible, just as the soul.

Procreation

Procreation is looked upon as a necessity (going by the Legend of Procreation). A man should have a woman to live with, as the Creator God of the Kherias created a male and a female. A person should not live alone—and hereby the concept of *'sanyasi life'* is negated. Man and Woman were initiated into sex act by Ponomoshor himself through an institution, which the Kherias believe was the first marriage on earth, presided over by Ponomoshor Himself. Therefore sex is not looked upon as ugly. However, having sex with someone who is not one's spouse is, however, not accepted, it is taken to be an offence. On the other hand, neither a man nor a woman should deprive his spouse of sex, if he or she desires it. However, sex mostly is for procreation.

Nature: Are Kherias Nature Worshippers?

Creation (Nature) holds a very significant place in the Munda worldview and philosophy. Going by the Legend of Creation, Singbonga appears to have created the Earth, and thereupon Nature, animals and birds for the Man, before He created the Man and the Woman, so that when the two come into being, they have a ready dwelling place and food. Among all the other creatures of creation, Singbonga created Man as the most intelligent, rational and thinking creature. However, he did not make Man the master of the creation, did not place the creation at his feet to do whatever he liked to do with it. He gave the creation to the Man to live in, assigned him a place whereby, being superior among other creatures in the creation, he should take care of them and keep them as they are. Kherias do not remember the Asur Kani, but they seem to believe in everything that the legend yields. When the Asurs started over-exploiting Nature for their greed and pride, he decided to set things in order. The grass, the trees and the herbs withered due to excessive heat of the furnace of the Asurs where they smelted iron day in and day out, in order to get richer and more powerful. The animals did not get water, because even the water sources were drying up, men did not get food and water because the fruit-bearing trees had been negatively affected by the environmental hazard caused by the excessive heat. This is why Singbonga decided to send message to the Asur thrice to amend their ways. But when the Asurs did not relent in their evil ways, Singbonga decided to destroy them.

Man in Vedic Philosophy

Man, according to the Vedas, is the result of the Gods' sacrifice of the divine primordial form of man. As a concept, it is also found among many other peoples, the parts of this first being became the various living creatures, including man.

The Rig Veda states, "Thousand-headed is the Man with a thousand eyes, a thousand feet; encompassing the Earth on all sides, he exceeded it by ten fingers' breath. That Man, indeed, is this All, what has been and what is to be, the Lord of the immortal spheres which he surpasses by consuming food. Such is the measure of his might, and greater still than this is Man. All beings are a fourth of him, three-fourths are the immortal in heaven. Using the Man as their oblation, the Gods performed the sacrifice. Thus evolved Man, then first born, they besprinkled on the sacred grass. With him, the Gods performed the sacrifice, as did also the heavenly beings and seers. From this sacrifice, fully accomplished, were born the hymns and the melodies; from this were born the sacrificial formulas. When they divided up the Man, his mouth became the brahmin; his arms became the warrior-prince, his legs the common man who plies his trade. The lowly serf was born from his feet. The Moon was born from his mind; the Sun came into being from his eye; from his mouth came Indra and Agni, while from his breath the Wind was born".[123]

Some thinkers like Swami Vivekananda, the greatest exponent of Vedanta in the western world, regard Man as Divine. The Vedas indicate so when they say the *Mahavakya 'Aham Brahmasmi'* (I am Brahman). The Varna-Ashrama-Purusartha concept of Vedic philosophy is argued to be helping man to achieve this divinity in him. While *Varna* concept has been discussed before, ashrama indicates the calling of man at his different stages of life: *brahmacharya, grihasthya, vanaprastha and sanyasa,* Purusartha (meaning of life) urges a Man to follow certain duty that includes Dharma, Artha, Kama and Moskha. The second and the third one have to be achieved and performed in order to do

Dharma, which ultimately is aimed to achieve Moksha. A Man is not allowed to secure artha by unfair means, he has to do so only by fair means (with Dharma). Further, he also has to pursue sexual pleasure which is necessary for his life, in an ethical way. In this, Man rises from animal to human level by accepting *pravritti* dharma i.e., by observing social injunctions. He ascends to godhood and becomes divine by embracing the *nivritti* dharma.

This Hindu concept of liberation, in turn, is based upon another concept of an ever pure, ever free, ever perfect, ever conscious spiritual entity in man called Atman (soul). According to the Vedas, this Atman is the Real Man as against the body-mind complex which is only the apparent man.

The relation between the real and apparent men has been beautifully described through an allegory in the Katha Upanishad:

"Know the soul to be the master of the chariot and the body the chariot. Consider the intellect the charioteer, and the mind the reins. The senses, they say, are the horses, and their roads are the sense objects. The wise call Him the enjoyer when He is united with the body, senses and mind."[124]

The Upanishads have further elaborated this concept by stating that the real Man or Atman is conscious, ever free, blissful and immortal. The apparent Man consists of five sheaths which cover the soul or Atman. These are (1) *annamaya kosha*, the physical body or the physical sheath, (2) *pranamaya kosha*, the vital sheath or the sheath life-force, (3) *manamaya kosha*, the mental sheath, (4) *vijnanamaya kosha*, the consciousness sheath, and (5) *anandamaya kosha*, the blissful sheath. Through these various stages sheaths, Atman (soul or self), makes progress towards Brahman (the Supreme Soul or the Universal Self).[125]

The Vedic Man also is one who offers sacrifices to gods regularly, performs yajnas, lives in the Cosmic and the Moral Order and believes that he is in bondage of birth, death and rebirth. His *karma* binds him in the eternal cycle of birth, death and rebirth and only *niskama karma* can help him detach himself from the cycle of rebirth. The asharama and Purusarthas are there for Man to liberate himself from rebirth.

Sex

The Vedantins discuss sex just as they discuss any other sacred subject like *Atman* or *Brahman*, in a pure and holy way, without showing any pejorative attitude towards it. For them, sex is a sacred thing that needs to be performed by every man. Upanishads equate sexual intercourse to *yajna*, giving it a position of a sacred work; a similarity could well be drawn up with Munda thought on sex mentioned before.

"From Him comes the Fire (i.e., the heavens), whose fuel is the sun; from the moon comes rain, the herbs that grow on the earth; from the herbs the seminal fuild which a man pours into a woman. Thus many living beings are born from the Purusha."[126]

"Day and night verily, are Prajapati. Of these, day is the eater, prana, and night the food. Those who join in sexual intercourse by day verily dissipate life; but to join in sexual intercourse by night is verily, chastity."[127] This kind of self-control is advised for the householder.

"This (person) is, at first, the germ in a man. That which is the semen is here called germ. This semen is the vigour (tejas) drawn from all the limbs. The man bears the self (i.e., the semen) in the self (i.e., the body). When he pours the semen into a woman, he gives it a birth. This, indeed, is the first birth of the embodied soul."[128]

"That semen becomes one with the woman—just like a limb of her own. That is why it does not hurt her. She nourishes this self of his that has come into her."[129]

These verses from *Aitereya Upanishad* highlight the sacredness of sexual intercourse in procreation. It also equates man's semen as his 'self' that gets born as a child through the woman who nourishes it. This is further reiterated in the *Brihadaranyaka Upanishad's* verse:

"He was not all happy. Therefore a person [even today] is not happy when alone. He desired a mate. He became the size of a man and wife in close embrace. He divided his body into two. From that [division] arose husband (pati) and wife (patni). Therefore, as Yajnavalkya said, the body [before one accepts a wife] is one-half of oneself, like the half of a split pea. Therefore this space is indeed filled by the wife. He was united with her. From that (union) human beings were born."[130]

Sexual intercourse is even equated to a yajna, as the following verse of Brihadaranyaka Upanishad suggests:

"Woman, O Gautama, is the fire, her sexual organ is the fuel, the hairs the smoke, the vulva the flame, the sexual intercourse the cinders, enjoyment the spark. In this fire the gods offer semen as oblation. Out of this offering a man is born. He lives as long as he is to live."[131] This again is repeated in Chhandogya Upanishad, 5.viii.1-2.

At other places, sex is discussed in detail, and as the highest level of sacrifice a man should perform, and often from the dominat male point of view. Women, it is feared, may not appreciate the way it should be, as the Vedantins probably originally meant.

"Prajapati said to Himself: 'Well, let Me make a firm basis for it (semen)'. So He created woman. Having created her, he placed her below and worshipped her. Therefore one should worship a woman, placing her below. He (Prajapati) extended His organ that projects and with it penetrated her."[132]

"He who, knowing this, practices sexual intercourse wins as great a world as is won through the Vajapeya sacrifice; he acquires for himself [the fruit of] the good deeds of the woman. But he who, without knowing this, practices sexual intercourse turns over to the woman his own good deeds."[133] Sex has such a sacred place in Hindu life that there is a treatese on this—*Kamasutra* of Vatsyayana, and temples have prominent sculptures on sex.

In the Munda way too, festivals mark celebrations of sun-earth's marriage which bears fruits and new life in the world. Sex for new life has always been regarded sacred and worshipped, as the myths narrated earlier shows. Worship is performed before the Munda farmer performs ploughing the earth every year before sowing seeds. The seed is taken to be the semen that falls on the ground and bears fruit. It is from this act of sowing seed that the Mundas will later develop the concept of rebirth that later would be incorporated in the Vedic philosophy[134]. Not only rebirth, things like domestication of animals and birds, word like 'Ganga', *sindur* (vermilion) on the forehead of the married woman, calculation of days observing the moon (*raka* and *kuhu: raka* for fullmoon and *kuhu* for new moon), flowing the ash of dead bodies in the river water, worship of trees, stones, hills etc, had their beginning with the Austro-Asiatic group, which later were assimilated by Vedic culture[135].

Christianity: From Akbar to Adivasis

Christianity in India began with St Thomas, a disciple of Jesus Christ coming to South India and preaching the Gospel. A few Brahmin families are said to have been the first ones to adopt the new faith. Later, Christianity spread into different parts of South India and then into North India. After St Thomas, St Francis Xavier was another notable Christian priest who came to India and left an indelible mark. Following him, a few Jesuit priests also were active in Goa in the Portugese settlement when Akbar the Great ruled Hindustan. Akbar was ever curious to learn new things and when he came to know about Jesuit priests preaching a new faith, he is supposed to have called one from 'Bengala' (whose name is not known), on whose advice three other

Jesuit priests from Goa were invited by Akbar to his court. 'Akbar sent a letter to the head of the Jesuits in Goa and he chose to send Father Rodolfe Aquauia, son of Duke of Atria, and Father Antonie de Monserrat and Father Francois Henriques'[136]. After the first Jesuit priest (whose name is not known) and the next batch of three Jesuit priests, there were more who lived with the Great Mogul and his succesors. The three Jesuits have left behind diaries, which was collected by Father Pierre Du Jarric, and a book titled 'Akbar and the Jesuits: An Account of the Jesuit Mission to the Court of Akbar,' was published by him in France between 1608 and 1614. The Jesuit priests in the court of Akbar tried to convert Akbar into Christianity and have written interesting diaries in the process. 'The Fathers who resided at the Mogul court were men of learning and culture and in most cases accomplished writers. They were also keen and shrewed; and as far as their religious prejudices permitted, sympathetic obsever. Had they therefore chosen to devote more attention and to write more fully of the concerns of the empire, their letters would have held a place the most valueable and the most authoritative of the world's historical records. But it was no part of their business to collect material for history of the reign of Akbar. Their mission was to convert the monarch to Christianity.'[137]

The Romans called India as *'India Citerior'* or *'India Inter Gangem'* (India on this side of the Ganges), which 'we call Indostan is today in the possession of a powerful monarch who is generally known as Great Mogor'[138]. The Jesuit priests spell Akbar as 'Eckebar, 'Achebar' or 'Aquebar'; and 'Hindustan' as 'Indostan' and 'Industan'. The missionaries' diaries say and Jarric writes: 'It was in the year 1582 that his court was first visited by the fathers of the Company. He was then about forty years of age; of medium stature, and strongly built. He wore a turban on his head, and the fabric of his costume was interwoven with gold thread. His outer garment reached to his knees, and his breaches to his heels. His stockings were much like ours, but his shoes were of a peculiar pattern invented by himself"[139]. Akbar, according to the missionaries, was melancholy by temperament and suffered from 'falling sickness'. He liked to watch cock fight to overcome melancholy[140]. Many kings attended Akbar's court, 'some of these kings are Pagans and others Mahometans; but Echebar, although he possessed Mahometan faith, placed more trust in the former than the later'[141]. At one point Akbar, according to the diaries of the missionaries, is believed to have pondered over seriously about Christianity. He heard the deliberations of the missionaries in the evident gladness; and 'so strongly was he moved to abandon his faith that, one evening while conversing with his Caziques or Mullas as the priests of the Mahometan religion are called, he told them frankly that he had decided to follow the counsel of the good priest, and pray to God for light to see the truth. At this discussion Soldan of Mecque [Mecca] the chief of all his Mullas or Caziques, was present, who the moment these words fell from the kings lips, said: "Your Majesty follows a good law and has no reason to doubt it or see another. On hearing this the king rose to his feet and exclaimed—May God help us. May God help us!"'[142] Akbar was a hard nut to crack and his did not allow his emotions to overpower his reason.

Thus the missionaries saw in 'this Prince the common fault of the atheist, who refuses to make reason subservient to faith, and accepting nothing as true, which his feeble mind is unable to fathom'[143]. He also had the habit of questioning; he would suddenly ask another question when a question is being answered and the missionaries found that 'he had not the patience to hear one explanation at a time'.[144] At one point of time when the missionaries were deliberating on their faith, Akbar appeared satisfied and told the Fathers that their Law 'seemed to him good,'[145] but that he desired them to explain to him 'the Mystery of the Holy Trinity, and how God could have a son who became a man'[146]. Lastly, Akbar had a great desire to witness a miracle, and several times 'he suggested that, to prove which of the two laws was the better, that of the Christians or that of the Saracens, the Fathers and the Mullas, the former holding their scriptures and later their Koran, should enter a fire together, and those who were not burnt should be regarded as the possessor of the true law,'[147] to which the missionaries and the mullas declined.

That Akbar did not place his faith in any religion has been proved beyond doubt, and that he had his own way of looking at religion and God or Supreme Power has many evidences. However, Akbar, according to the missionaries, was an ardent worshipper of the Sun. He would listen to the discourse on the Christian faith, but show no sign of abandoning his 'superstitious worship of the Sun, which he adored everyday at sunrise and an image of which he kept constantly near him',[148] to 'whose worship Akbar was addicted'[149].

After more than two centuries when the new political situation in India had obliterated the memories of the three great Moguls—greatly contributed by the fourth Mogul ruler, and the British had replaced them, missionaries arrive among the tribes in Central Indian regions. Christianity among the Mundas began in November 1845 with the arrival of the members of a Missionary Society, founded by John Baptist Gossner in Germany, in Chotanagpur. Through Calcutta, they came to Ranchi and established mission stations in Domba and Govindpur. For five years until 1850, they received lukewarm response from the Mundas and the Oraons of Chotanagpur. In June 1850, they got their first break when four Oraons[150], who had come to Ranchi for their court cases, were baptised[151]. The Mundas [here the Kompat Mundas] were more conservative and they were slow to receive anything new. The first of the Munda tribe being baptised is recorded in November 1851[152]. In the days to come, the first converts further brought their kin and relatives to Ranchi to be instructed and baptised. Tribes from adjascent villages too followed their examples and conversion went steadily. 'The new converts realised that the new faith brought some distinct temporal advantages. The Christian was freed from the dreaded fear of malevolent spirits (bonga) and sorcerers; he no longer had to pay for sacrifice and the magician; he could with impunity take wood from the *sarnas*, and he felt stronger in his struggle against landlords'[153].

The rapid growth of the Mission was temporarily checked by the Revolt of 1857, when the Eurpoean missionaries, for reason of safety had to leave Chotanagpur for Calcutta.

During this time an internal conflict among missionaries confused the converted Christian tribes. A few Lutheran missionaries left the older mission and became Anglican, and after coming back to Ranchi from Calcutta, they started re-converting Lutheran Christians into Anglican. On the administrative side, a change was going to come and it came in 1869 when British promulgated Bhuihari Survey and Settlement Act, 1869.

Prior to this in 1867, some Christians complained to the Commissioner of Chotanagur Col. Dalton against the oppression by the landlords, ejection of tenants, exorbitant rent and refusal of the landlords to give receipt of rent paid etc. asking the authorities to stop all these. The Commissioner, suspecting that the Christians were agitators, rejected the petition; following which the petion was sent by the Christians to Lieutenant Governor in Calcutta. The Christian missionaries informed the Government that the issues raised in the petition was correct. Following this the Bhuinhari Survey and Settlement Act, 1869 was made.

The people, however, were suspicious of the intention of the British Government, and were not willing to declare their property. The missionaries saw that this reluctance of the tribes will cost them dearly of their rightful Bhuinhari lands, they took it upon themselves and asked the people to declare their Bhuinhari lands for survey-settlement. Some did, but many non-Christians did not; they omitted to stake claim on their land and those lands were lost for ever. Some Christians also lost their land as they, suspecting the intention of the British, did not put their claim. The non-Christians, who had lost their land, thought it was the conspiracy of the Christian missionaries; while the Christians who had not staked claim on their land and hence lost them, too, thought it due to the Christian missionaries. Some Christians put exorbitant claims, which obviously appeared false. The British administrators thought that the false claims made were to the wrong information put out by the Christian missionaries about the Act. Thus, the poor Christian missionaries were on the receiving end from all sides.

The movement of the people that begun in 1867 and the Act of 1869 failing to redress, was the beginning of Sardari Movement, so called because the leaders of the movement were mostly Munda sardars, now converted into Christianity. This movement later would give birth to Birsa Munda, who will in days to come wage an Ulgulan Movement against the British, giving up Christian faith that he was initially baptised into.

Christianity was adopted by many Mundas and Oraons and as the missionaries set up schools and colleges, the new faith also brought education in the society, not just for the converted Christians but for others in the region too. Education produced many great men among Mundas, most important among them being Jaipal Singh, who received his education in London and coming back to Chotanagpur played an important role in giving the tribes a new identity when India was about to enter a new phase after the British had decided to depart.

Christianity traces its origin to Jesus Christ of Nazareth, a philosopher the Christians worship as God or Son of

God; and Islam regards as a Prophet, Messenger of God. Christianity is an Abrahamic religion and is an offshoot of Judaism, one of the ancient religions of the world. The Bible is the holy scripture of the Christians, with two parts: the Old Testament and the New Testament. While the Old Testament consists of four parts: i) The Pentateuch, ii) The Historical Books, iii) The Wisdom Books, and iv) the Prophets; the New Testament is the description of life, work and sermons of Christ and his disciples.

The Old Testament's first book: The Pentateuch, is further divided into five books—i) Book of Genesis, ii) Book of Exodus, iii) Book of Leviticus, iv) Book of Numbers, and v) Book of Deutoronomy. Collectively, these five books are called *Torah* or the Law. The Book of Genesis is the most read and discussed of books in the Old Testament, in that it deals with the God (Yahweh), Origin of the World, and Origin of the Human race. Most scholars regard it as stories to point to the creative work of Yahweh God, while majority of believers, just like in other religious traditions with their respective stories, think that the stories are true. In any case, with regard to religious traditions, it is the stories that seem to be believed more than real hard facts.

There are many versions of the Bible, and each differs with the other in tone and narration. For the work at hand, *The Jerusalem Bible* (Standard Edition, Darton, Longman and Todd Ltd, UK) has been chosen to study and quote. This is for two reasons: first, The Jerusalem Bible is regarded as the closest English translation from the original Bible written in Hebrew; and second, because with large number of footnotes that help a researcher to understand the actual context that prevailed while the Bible was being written down in words, this version of the Bible is edifying. Here after, *The Jerusalem Bible* would be referred to as *the Bible* in the entire work.

The Yahweh God of Judaism is basically the God experience that the Jewish people with Abraham as their forefather, experienced during their lifetime. Over the years, this God experience became systematised and institutionalised, with rites and rituals, temples and traditions. Institutions of priests also came up who crafted and drafted religious rites everyday, converting Yahweh and God into an alien supernatural only to be mediated by them, for the ordinary believer. There appeared a huge gap between Yahweh God and the believer, and the gap now could be filled only by the priest, who charged the believer heavily in the name of rendering sundry religious services.

Meanwhile, the Jews, who had been brought under by different rulers at different point of time, including the Great Roman Empire, were looking for a Messiah, a 'hero' who the Yahweh God had promised to send for them to liberate them from the shackles of slavery. Judaism too, had completely become personal business of the priestly class of the Jewish society and the ordinary folk were alienated and even persecuted at will. It is in this background that Jesus was born in Nazreth, Jeusalem, with a new philosophy, the philosophy of love and forgiveness that eventually caught the imagination of the people.

Jesus is not a de-link from the Old Testament, from the past philosophical and religious tradition of the Jews; in fact he establishes link with it. Thus the life of Jesus: *The New Testament*; and the past philosophical tradition of the Jews: *The Old Testament*; forms one complete religio-philosophical tradition. In order to understand the concept God and Man in Christianity, one has to begin from the Old Testament.

Christian Man

According to Christian philosophy, man is the supreme creature in the creation of God. Man is created in the *'likeness'* of God, but not as god, and given the right to rule over the creation and other creatures of the Creation by none other than God Himself. It is due to this philosophy that Man can use or misuse anything in the Creation or any creature, as he wishes. Man can destroy things at will, because Man is the *'master'*, and not the *'caretaker'*. The origin of things like consumerism—using natural resources for one's gratification, and the attitude of *'winning Nature'* (discovering the space, sky, sea, waters, mountain tops etc) in the followers of Christian philosophy comes naturally from this background.

Woman is created after Man, as part of Man in Christian philosophy. Hence, the concept of gender equality in Christian philosophy is not natural, and mostly an alien concept, though tradition of free philosohical thought of the present day has moved thinkers for concepts like gender equality. Woman is an alibi labelled as 'instigator' of Man to do things prohibited by God through commandments. Man is the loved one of God, while Woman is the loved one of Man—'this one at last is bone of my bones and flesh of my flesh'[154].

Man is also thought of in Christian philosophy as 'fallen' from the grace of God, and he has to abide by the teachings of 'Son of God' to redeem himself. This act of God sending the 'Son' to redeem the 'people' is thought to be an act of love and mercy, forgiveness and kindness. And these virtues, further, have to be practised by the people adhering to Christian philosophical tradition.

The Christian view of man is rooted in Christ, the ultimate model of human perfection. Each person, created in the image and likeness of God, is bestowed with dignity, freedom, intellect, and will, just as the first man Adam was bestowed with. These endowments have to be brought out by education—this is what Christian education pedagogy is centred around.

Man is thought to be nothing vis-a-vis God, his Creator. However Christian philosophy attributes the element of 'divineness' in man, just as the Vedas do. This can be seen when King David sings this psalm, pondering over man's insignificance:

"When I consider Thy heavens, the work of Thy fingers, the moon and the stars, which Thou hast ordained; What is man, that Thou dost take thought of him? And the son of man, that Thou dost care for him? Yet Thou hast made him a little lower than God, and dost crown him with glory and majesty! Thou dost make him to rule over the works of Thy hands; Thou hast put all things under his feet…"[155] (Psalm 8:3-6). In the same breath, another Biblical character, Job, says, "What is man that Thou dost magnify him, and that Thou art concerned about him?"[156] God is Self-existent, and man exists because God created him. God is Creator, and man is the creature. Thereby a necessary distinction between the Creator and the creation is maintained. Man is not God, nor can he become, as promised in the Vedas with the mahavakya *'Aham Brahmasmi' (I am God)*. Nor does man function as God, or even as a "co-god." When God created man, He created *out of* Himself, that which *was not* Himself. God, according to Christian philosophy is a Personal God, in that He is a Person with personal attributes. The Christian God is in Trinitarian relational Personhood, in which Father, Son and the Holy Spirit are intricately related. However, though Christian God has attributes, He is a Spirit, an Infinite Mind and Being that pervades everything, time and space. It is due to this nature that God existed when nothing, including Man, did. Matter is limited and Spirit is not. And as Christian God is not limited, He is pure Spirit.

God is immortal and eternal[157], and "alone possesses immortality"[158]. What God is, man is not. Man is physically mortal, and "It is appointed unto man to die…."[159] On the other hand, Man is a *creature* created by the Creator God. Man is a *personal creature* – not essential Personhood as God alone is, but a personal creature capable of interpersonal relationships with God and with other men. Man is a *social creature*, who needs both God and other people. Man cannot live alone, just as the first man could not and required a woman to live with. But woman is a 'helper' of man, according to Christian philosophy, and not a mate, 'But no helper suitable for the man was found for him. The Yahweh God made the man fall into a deep sleep. And while he was asleep, he took one of his ribs and closed the flesh up again forthwith. Yahweh god fashioned the rib he had taken from the man into a woman, and brought her to the man."[160]

Christian philosophy does not differentiate one man from another on the basis of creation, like the Vedas propagate. While there can be philosophically inherent gender inequality in it, there is equality in men. However, the concept of racial inequality that has crept into the practioners of Chritsian religious tradition in the West and African nations, is due to non-philosophical matter, due to 'power-play' than due to philosophical issues.

Christian Apple and Munda Sex

God existed before anything else did. He 'created the heaven and the earth'[161]. Heaven was created, and heaven is a creation of God, just as earth is. The earth, the Genesis speaks, was a *formless void*, and 'there was darkness over the deep, with a divine wind sweeping over the waters'[162]. It is not known whether water was created by God or it existed before. But as God is said by Genesis to have created the *earth*, it is inferred that God created *earth with water* in it.

God then created the day and the night, the morning and the evening. God also separated the 'waters' into one place and the *'dry land'* appeared. This dry land became the 'earth' and the waters became the 'seas'[163].

God then created the vegetation, birds, animals, aquatic creatures and all that now exist on the 'earth' and in the 'seas'. He then decided that He should create Man. "Let *us* create Man in *our* own image, in the likeness of *ourseleves*,"[164] He said. The plural words *us*, *our* and *ourselves* arouse curiosity. While this version of the Bible says that God must have consulted *others* in His court, it also alternatively says that the 'common name for God in Hebrew is *elohim*, a plural form. However, if one goes by another verse in the Bible 'God knows in fact that the day you will eat it, your eyes will be opened and you will be like *gods*, knowing good from evil'[165], indicates that there were other *gods* in the court of God, placing a question on the avowed monotheistic tradition of Christianity, raising possibility of initial polytheism. The gods must have been tutelary gods just like the Hindusim's or the *bongas* (spirits) of the Munda religious tradition.

God created Man. And upon Man's creation, God says 'Let them be the masters of the fish of the sea, the birds of heaven, the cattle, all the wild animals and all the creatures that creep along the ground'[166]. It is important to note here that Man is positioned by God as the *master* of other creatures. Other creatures of creation, thus, are at the foot of Man to serve, to be used at will, the way Man may deem fit. Man is the *Master* of Creation, not its *'caretaker'*, as in case of Munda philosophy.

God, after creating the creatures and Man, gives Man a 'command'—not to eat the fruit of a tree that stood in the middle of the Garden of Eden. But soon God had to realise that Man was feeling lonely, and required another person to be with him. God then made the Man fall in deep slumber and took one of his ribs, and created a Woman from it. Woman, thus, came (was created) *after* the Man, and positioned only next to Man in all the Abrahamic relious traditions. However, Man calls Woman as 'bone of my bones and flesh of my flesh,'[167] and 'becomes attached to his wife'[168]. The point is similar to the Vedic concept where Man becomes twice his size and divides himself into two, the other being the woman he takes as wife. In both the cases of the Vedic and Abrahamic traditions, Man and Woman are ever eager to become *'one'* again, naturally, without even having the trace of this traditional legend. In the Munda philosophical tradition, however, man and woman were born from the eggs—according to Santal tradition, and live like companions. They have to be induced into sex by God Himself, and natural sense of *'becoming one'* (copulation) does not arise.

Man disobeys the 'commands' of Yahweh God and the Yahweh God drives the couple out of the Garden of Eden, to toil the land and grow edible foodgrains and live. This shows thar Yahweh God has personal attributes. He gets angry, just like human beings; He punishes disobedience or mistakes. Yahweh God is a Creator God who can 'create out of nothing'. The Creation story of the Book of Genesis in the Old Testament, does not mention whether the primordial stuffs were present or not. But the way the Creation story of Genesis talks, one feels that these were non-existent; only God existed, and with Him, the gods too. God, however, in later books, through the Prophets, proclaims that He will 'redeem' His people fallen in sin, through a *Messiah.* Thus, the Christian God has also the attributes of love, mercy and kindness. This, the study of New Testament reveals, gets manifested with the coming of Jesus Christ, and with his teachings.

Another important subject in the concept of God in Christianity is the point of godhead: the *Trinity*, three gods in one: Father, Son and the Holy Spirit. This concept emerges in the New Testament. Jesus calls himself as the *'Son of God'* and promises to send the *'Holy Spirit'* among his disciples.

God *is* Self-existent, and man exists because God created him. God is Omnipotent, Omnipresent and Omniscient. God is Creator, and man is the creature.

God is Self-sufficient. No one outside of God influences or controls His actions. God is unconditioned, un-contingent, and unconstrained. God is Autonomous and Independent. He is a law unto Himself. He is His own centre of reference. God is "Independent Self". He creates without anything outside Himself. God can act 'out of nothing'—*ex-nihilo*, He is the Almighty and Absolute Being, who can will something to happen. A Pure Spirit, He wills His *'will'* to transform it into 'matter'. Thus, the Christian's God's creative power is a 'spirit' being able to 'become matter'.

The concept of sex is the most untouchable subject in Christian philosophy. Unlike the Vedic philosophy and the Munda philosophy where it can be discussed with some degree of sacredness and good intension, Christian philosophy does not enjoy this openness. Ironically, however, adherents of the philosophical traditions are just the opposite in their outlook towards sex as compared to the tenets that their respective philosophies propound. The adherents of Christian philosophy are far too open on matters of sex though their philosophy propounds secrecy. Opposite is the case with the adherents of the Vedic philosophy though the Vedas are highly candid on the subject. With regard to Munda philosophy on sex, they are neither too open nor too closed, probably keeping the philosophical tradition in toto.

"It asked the women, 'Did God really say you were not to eat from any of the trees in the garden? The woman answered the snake, 'We may eat the fruit of the trees in the garden. But the fruit of the tree in the middle of the garden God said, 'You must not eat it, nor touch it, under pain of death'."[169]

This passage is oridinarily believed by the laymen to be symbolically talking of sex while no one knows whether it is symbolic or not. Though some scholars opine that it actually talked of *'knowledge or awareness'*, the next verse—'Then the eyes of both of them were opened and they realised that they were naked'[170]—makes one feel that sexual knowledge was all dawned on the first couple first. 'So they sewed fig-leaves together to make themselves loin clothes'[171]. Unlike the Munda philosophical legends, the Bible does not talk about how the man and the woman got initiated into the sexual act. From the verse, "The man had intercourse with his wife Eve, and she conceived and gave birth to Cain"[172], sex came naturally to them, after knowledge of *'nakedness'* had dawned upon them with the eating of the forbidden fruit.

Soul from Greece

Even as we are conscious of the broad and very common Biblical usage of the term "soul," one must be clear that scripture does not present even a rudimentarily developed concept of the 'soul'. The creation narrative is clear that all life originates with God, yet the scripture offers no specific understanding of the origin of 'individual soul', of when and how it becomes attached to specific body, or of its potential existence, apart from the body, after death. The reason for this is that, as we noted at the beginning, the Hebrew Bible—the Book of Genesis and other books, does not present a theory of the soul. "Yahweh God shaped man from the soil of the ground and blew the breath of life into his nostrils, and man became a living being"[173]. The important thing here is to notice is that God placed into the man the *'breath of life'*, which actually is *'life-force' (respiration)*, and not *'soul'* (Atman). There is no initial concept of 'immortal soul' and even when Cain, the first born of the first couple—Adam and Eve upon their sexual intercourse[174], is born and kills his brother Abel, there is no discussion of what 'soul' is. "Cain set on his brother Abel and killed him. Yahweh asked Cain, "'Where is your brother Abel?' 'I do not know,' he replied"'[175]. This was the first death to occur, and neither did Cain, if we go strictly by the scripture, know that that the life breath of Abel would end. If the Hebrews who lived by the scripture had any concept of soul (Atman), the scripture would have discussed what happened to Abel (or what happened to the 'soul' of Abel) after his death. This absence of discussion over soul (Atman) is much in line with mere 'life-energy' or 'life-force' or 'life-breath' that Yahweh God put into Adam, the first man; without a clue of the concept of an eternal soul. "Herod sought Jesus' soul."[176] The verse, which is in the New Testament, also does not mean the 'immortal soul'. All it means is *'life-breath'* or *'life'*. Herod, the king wanted to kill Jesus, who he thought will usurp his kingdom. Herod certainly did not want the immortal soul of Jesus, but wanted the *life* of Jesus. Thus, even in the initial phase of Christianity, the Christian philosophy does not have the concept of 'immortal soul' (Atman). 'Soul' may refer to the 'whole person', the self: 'three thousand souls' were converted,'[177] Here the word 'soul' simply means 'individuals or 'persons'.

"But the Jew did not believe that human beings consist of an immortal soul entombed for a while in a mortal body."[178]

"While the idea of an immortal soul is an established belief for most Christians, it cannot be supported by Biblical texts."[179]

In the Old Testament Hebrew people did not have any concept of soul in the sense of the Vedic Atman, the New Testament, however, has verses which prove that the concept of soul had emerged. "Do not be afraid of those who kill the body but cannot kill the soul; fear him rather who can destroy both body and soul in hell"[180]. This simply means that Jesus was talking about body and soul as two different entities. Soul, however, according to Jesus, was destructible, at least by God. This stands in complete contrast to the Vedic and Munda understanding of the soul, which say that soul is indestructible and survives the destruction of the body. Jesus himself, thus, never discussed soul as Atman, immortal, eternal and indestructible, but spoke of *soul* only as a different entity from the *body*.

However, it is in the later philosophers in later times that one can notice the present understanding of 'soul', *somewhat but not fully*, develops in Christian philosophy, as can be seen from this verse of St Luke in his Gospel, 'Anyone who wants to save his life will lose it; but anyone who loses his life for my sake, will save it. What benefits it to anyone to win the whole world and forfeit or lose his very *self*?"[181] Here, the *self* undoubtedly means the concept of 'soul', which does not die but gets the reward or punishment in accordance with the work of the individual. It is not meant in the original Hebrew sense of 'life-breath' or 'life-force'. Probably when St Luke was writing his Gospel, which was believably done several years after the death of Christ when the teachings of Christ had already gathered a large number of followers, and had become a 'way' on the path of becoming a 'religion' after being its practices institutionalised. It is suggested that this development in the understanding of soul as different from 'life force or 'life breath', and as 'immortal' was the result of the Greek philosophy's influence in Christianity. Greek philosophers such as Socrates, Plato and Aristotle understood that soul is an 'immortal substance' and that which survives the bodily destruction, enumerated in the last book of his *magnum opus*.[182] They attributed soul to have logical faculty, the exercise of which was the most divine of human actions. Soul, according to them, had other faculties like reason, character, feeling, consciousness, memory, perception and thinking. "According to Plato, the individual soul is a part of the universal soul and resembles it in all respect."[183] The only difference between the two is that the individual soul is less perfect than the universal soul. Plato further believed in the 'Tripartite theory of the soul', in that he believed that soul has three parts: *rational soul, noble irrational soul and ignoble irrational soul*. But Plato again believes in the 'indivisibility' of soul[184]. Divisibility is not possible without destruction, and destruction of soul is not possible, the soul according to Plato is simply *indestructible*. It is immortal; Plato's 'soul' does not suffer death and destruction[185].

Later, Christian philosophers, particularly Plotinus, St Augustine and St Thomas fully developed the concept of 'soul' which had entered into their religious tradition due to the influence of Greek philosophy. According to Plotinus, "Soul is of divine nature, man's aim in life is to rise above the sentiment world and live in divine presence"[186]. As for St Augustine, soul is 'simple and immaterial' and is 'altogether different in nature from the nature of the body. Augustine leaves the question of the origin of soul unsettled, though he denies the pre-existence of soul".[187] Augustine gives three possible ways of explaining the origin of soul[188]: i) God creates a new soul for every child that is born, ii) Souls are generated from the Souls of the parents, and iii) Eternal nature of the soul is undemonstrable, it is an act of faith. Augustine's concept of soul gives rise to logical problems such as, if the individual soul has an origin, it should have a death as well; for every alpha has an omega; and that if a child gets his soul from parents, soul is 'divisible'—which stands in contrast to the Vedic and Munda soul's 'indivisibility'; and finally he takes refuge in faith.

The 'origin of the soul' has provided a vexing question in Christianity. The first theory of its proponent St Augustine is known as *'Creationism'*, while the second is called *'Traducianism'* and the third *'Pre-existence'*. According to *Creationism*, each individual soul is created directly by God, either at the moment of conception or at some later time. According to *Traducianism*, the soul comes from the parents by natural generation. According to the *Pre-existence* theory, the soul exists before the moment of conception. But these are only possibilities that have been enumerated, and the very enumeration suggests a lack of 'definiteness' on the part of St Augustine. The theory of *Pre-existence* of souls, which thus is held by the Vedas, Bible and Munda philosophy, in any case, has to explain the population growth of the world in teeming millions.

St Thomas Aquinas, another great Christian philosopher, too, maintains that the soul is capable of existing apart from the living body after the death of the body, because the soul is 'incorruptible'. The full argument for the immortality of the soul and Aquinas' elaboration of Aristotelian theory is found in the First Part of the *Summa Theologica*, the best known work of Aquinas. This soul is in some contrast to the Vedic soul. '*na jayate mriyate va kadacin nayam bhutva bhavita va na bhuyah 'ajo nityah shasvato yam purano 'na hanyate hanyamane sharire.*'[189]

(For the atman there is neither birth nor death at any time. He has not come into being, does not come into being, and will not come into being. He is unborn, eternal, ever – existing and primeval. He is not slain when the body is slain.)

❑

CHAPTER 6

The Creator and Creation

God as Creation

Nanga Baiga nailed the Earth

In the beginning there was water, and God roamed over it. He thought it is not good to live alone. I should make the Earth. He created the Earth and placed it on the petals of a huge Lotus that floated on the water. But the Sun emitted cruel heat and the petals of the Lotus dried up. Down went the Earth into the deep waters. Thereafter, God made an Earth out of *lac*. But when he walked over it, it broke into pieces. Then he decided to make a Crow out of the flesh of his chest and said to it: "You have been fed with the milk of my breast; you will never feel thirsty or hungry. Both of us will now go in search of the Earth".

For many days and many nights, the Crow flew and flew around with God, looking for Earth, until one day he got very tired. He thought: “My own father has become my deadly enemy; he wants to kill me”. He could no longer fly. His head spun and he fell down. When he opened his eyes he saw that he had fallen on a Huge Crab, named Kekadmal Chatri. With the Crab on its back, Kekadmal Chatri went into the deep waters where he spotted King Nal and Queen Nal, both in deep slumber. They had been asleep for twelve years. Kekadmal Chatri shook both of them vigorously and awakened them. When they had opened their eyes, he asked them: “Where have you hidden the Earth?” “I haven't seen the Earth?” King Nal said. Hearing this, Kekadmal Chatri squeezed his throat and kept doing so until he ejected the Earth through his mouth. Then, the Crow caught the Earth and flew back to his father, the God. God then started giving final shape to Earth as he wanted.

The Earth used to always run around. After five years, Nanga Baiga and Nanga Baigin were born from a crack of the Earth. Nanga Baiga asked the Earth: “Mother, where is my Beena (a musical instrument)?” “Son, you have just been born! Why do you need a Beena?” asked Mother Earth.

On that same day, Basin (Bamboo) was born from another crack of the Earth at a distant place. Nanga Baiga sensed it. He went to the Basin and chopped it from below and from above. He then took out some hairs from his head and made the Beena and started playing it. The music emanating from the Beena shook the throne of God, and God learnt that Nanga Baiga had been born. He sent his messenger to call Nanga Baiga. When the messenger reached where Nanga

Baiga was, he found that Nanga Baiga was sleeping on a fan made of bamboo. Mother Earth said: "Son, don't go". But Nanga Baiga said: "Mother, let me go". He picked up his Beena and set out to meet God. When Nanga Baiga reached God, God looked at him and said: "Baiga, make a sharp nail and pierce it through the Earth. The Earth keeps running all the time". Nanga Baiga first made a nail out of bamboo and hit it into the Earth. But the Earth's run was too strong, and the bamboo nail could not bring Earth to a standstill. Nanga Baiga then cut his small finger and pierced the Earth with it. The Earth shook and came to a standstill. But God said, "I want a strong pillar to permanently keep the Earth fixed".

Nanga Baiga sat on a puja and worshipped Agneyasur (the Fire). Fire came with a strong blaze and out it was born an Agaria. The Agaria knew how to make iron ore. He smelted the iron ore and made 12 sharp virgin iron pillars. Nanga Baiga took those sharp iron pillars and pierced through the Earth, fixing her run forever. God then sowed seeds everywhere on the Earth, which grew into food grains. God then proceeded to create Man and Woman to live on Earth.

(The folktale is narrated by the Agarias, collected by Verrier Elwin in his book: *The Agarias*)

*

Singbonga is the *Creator* God indefinitely creating. But, the elements of water, earth (soil), air, ether and sky are pre-existent; and it is out of these things that Singbonga creates new things. These elements can be termed *'primordial elements'* even for Munda philosophy—just as in other philosophical traditions, and Munda philosophy holds that primordial elements are *not created*, they are self-existing and eternal. Just as Singbonga existed from the beginning, the primordial elements existed from the beginning. On this point, Munda philosophy draws a parallel with the Vedic philosophy in that it is held that the five elements (Panchatatva) existed from the beginning. But, Singbonga is a Creator who creates as per the needs of the human beings, just as he created day and night when he saw that man worked without rest[190]. According to Munda tradition, *dance (susun)* and *song (durang)* too were created by Singbonga for man so that after the hard work of the day, he relaxes in the evening as a community. Singbonga created different forms of *susun* (dance) and *durang* (song) for different seasons. Thus, a Munda sings a particular kind of *durang* and dances a particular form of *susun* during *sowing* and another set of *susun* and *durang* during harvest. So goes the dance and the song forms for seasons like spring, summer, rain etc.

The Vedic philosophy on Creation is originally found in the Purushasukta, and all other verses that speak of creation just follow from here. In it the *Purusha* was the origin, which begets all other things in creation[191]. In the Vedic philosophy too, the original Panchatatva (five primordial elements) are as eternal as the *Purusha*. Purusha can be equated to Yahweh or Singbonga God, or the *alpha*, from where evolves all other things in the universe.

Yahweh, unlike Singbonga, creates *ex-nihilo* (out of nothing). The Christian philosophy thus holds the view that something can be created out of nothing. Or *Matter* can be created out of *Pure Spirit*, if Yahweh is *Pure Spirit*—and He usually is believed to be so in Christian philosophy. Can matter be created by pure spirit? This has been a topic of philosophical debate and philosophers have opined 'no'. Because, matter limits, and spirit is not limited. No *limited* thing can come from an *unlimited* thing. So matter—world, should not come from spirit. And if the world (matter) has come from Yahweh God—or world (matter) has been created by Yahweh God *ex-nihilo*, then Yahweh God has in Him both *matter* and *spirit*—which is a view not held by Christian philosophy. Anything which is both matter and spirit, is both *limited* and *unlimited*. But, something is either *limited*, or it is *unlimited*. Thus, absence of five elements (primordial elements) in the beginning, and Yahweh god creating them as well as the world out of nothing (*ex-nihilo*) seems to carry a philosophical inconsistency.

Singbonga does not create caste system in the way Purusha does: *Brahman, Kshatriya, Vaisya* and *Sudra*. Singbonga does not create the institution of *pahan* (priest) in the Mundas, the institution of *pahan* is pre-existent. "He replied that if they [asur women] were obedient, the Mundari *pahan* would offer them [asur women] who become tutelary spirits—*bongas*) sacrifices."[192] Thus, in Munda philosophy, the institution of *pahan*, which had evolved at the very point of time when Singbonga created the humans and the world, gets revalidated by Singbonga himself. The ruler in the Munda race, usually known as *Munda—the head or chief*, however, had its origination socially. History suggests that this institution of *Munda (chief)* in the Munda group was more by virtue of democratic election and by consensus, than by the hereditary principle. The best—morally, socially, intellectually and physically, got elected as the Munda. If his elder son carried these qualities, he was appointed by the community elders to succeed his father. If not, a general election was called for. In recent days too, the institution of *Munda* of the village people in Munda group, is still prevalent and the position has come to become mere *symbolic* and often hereditary. There is no system of discrimination or social inequality on the basis of work division among people, and men of the entire Munda group (Kompat Munda, Santhal, Ho, Kharia, Bhumij and others) stand on the same footing with each other. But kinship rivalry among the groups is an open secret. They fight more among themselves than they fight their enemies.

Saguna (Personal) God or Nirguna (Impersonal) God

Singbonga, the Munda God, is a Personal God (*saguna*). He alone is the God—the Supreme Spirit, who hovered over the waters in the beginning, and it is He who created the tutelary spirits—the *bongas*, which, on His behalf, take care of different things like rivers, hills, land, stones, groves etc. Singbonga has attributes like love, kindness, forgiveness, fellow-feeling, anger etc; the qualities which too are found in the Mundas. In fact, these human qualities come to a Munda from the Singbonga himself. Anyone who has the highest and noblest of these qualities is regarded as the best man in the community, slated to become the chief (*the Munda*) and rule over others. Singbonga is a Spirit, but can take the form of flesh and blood just as He did when He came down to destroy the Asurs who had displeased Him by incessant iron-smelting that heated up the world. Singbonga can reward or punish a person, and the reward or punishment is on the basis of good work or bad work. Things like greed, jealousy, greedy use of natural resources, personal accumulation of natural resources etc, are regarded as bad work. On the other hand, good work is when a person lives the life of love, kindness and fellow-feeling. Singbonga can take Incarnation—which he did only once when he came down to the earth to set things in Order when the Asurs heated up the world by round-the-clock iron-smelting—but He usually likes not to. Mundas, unlike the adherents of Vedic philosophy, do not worship the Incarnated Singbonga. They worship Singbonga who lives in *sirma* (heaven). On special occasions, Singbonga comes down to the Earth, and usually his abode on the Earth is a *Sal* or *Sakhua* tree (Shorea robusta). It is due to this reason that the *pahan* sets up his place of worshipping Singbonga at the foot of a *sal* tree. He does not worship or offer sacrifices to the *sal* tree, but he worships and offers sacrifices to Singbonga who comes down and sits on the *sal* tree as the *pahan* invokes His name. The ordinary eye sees the *pahan* worshipping the tree (*sal* tree) and incorrectly terms Mundas as Animists. Mundas are monotheists and Singbonga tradition is monotheism. But, in as much as Singbonga is worshipped at the foot of a tree (*sal* tree), Mundas can also be termed animists. Animism is a belief that spirit of God can live in Nature. In the Munda philosophy, the spirit of Singbonga does live in a tree when He is invoked by the *pahan* to come down and take His place on a *sal* tree, and receive the sacrifices. Mundas thus are *preeminently* monotheistic, and secondarily animists. Mundas are not pantheists; they do not believe that the world is the spirit of Singbonga. Singbonga, in no case, is Sun God, and intellectuals who equate Him with Sun God—which many do—have only a remote knowledge of Munda philosophy. Sun is only a creation of Singbonga, just like any other creations in the world[193]. How can a created thing be Singbonga? the Mundas ask. This misconception of Sun regarded as Singbonga comes from the word *singi* (meaning *sun*). The word for Munda God is Singbonga and *not* Singibonga. The Mundas however respect the sun as one of the most powerful objects of creation residing in the sky, and may sometimes offer him their respect. This again makes it appear that Mundas are worshippers of the *sun*. When a salutation is raised towards the sun, it is not the sun that is worshipped; it is the *Singbonga that is.*

Singbonga, thus, is the *Saguna Brahman*, the *Ishvara* (apara-Brahman) of the Vedic philosophy. In it He has personal qualities and attributes. But Mundas do not worship any form, neither do they set up any idol (like that of Rama or Krishna—both Personal God with attributes, of the Vedic philosophy) for Singbonga. Neither do they conceive any form, let along convert it into an idol. This may make one feel that Mundas are worshipping the *Nirguna, Nirvishesa* and *Nirvachya*—para-Brahman. But, Singbonga is *Saguna, Savishesha* and *Vachya,* though He is not worshipped in his form, and worshipped as formless God, coming down and residing on the trees upon being invoked by the *pahan.*

Munads hold the view that this Singbonga, the *Ishvara* with personal attributes and qualities, existing without any form as a pure spirit with the ability to assume form, sits on a sal tree to receive their worship, sacrifice and oblations, keeping a vigil upon all of them every second. Thus, Munda Singonga is a *Nirakar-Saguna-Ishvara*, unlike the *Akar-Saguna-Ishvara* (apara-Brahman) of Vedic tradition. The Mundas hold the view that as mortal human beings, to conceive a *form* for Singbonga, would be an unintelligible attempt. The concept of *para-Brahma* of the Veda is non-existing in the Munda philosophy in as much as para-Brahman is described as *Nirguna*, *Nirvishesa* and *Nirvachya*, not keeping much interest in the affairs of the world. Singbonga keeps keen interest in the affairs of the world and the humans, and even regulates them with close monitoring.

Singbonga is similar to Yahweh God in all essence—who is Ishvara (para-Brahman of Vedic philosophy) with all attributes.

One question however arises here when similarities are sought to be seen in Singbonga and para-Brahman (Ishvara) of the Vedic tradition. The question is: 'When Singbonga sits on the sal tree, does the sal tree become a *form*, for Singbonga? Or when He sits on other objects of the Nature and the Mundas worship Him at the foot of the Nature, does Singbonga convert Himself to Nature?' This problem is similar to the problem of *Brahma-vivarta-vada* of Sankara and *Brahma-parinama-vada* of Ramanuja. Which of these—*Brahma-vivarta-vada* or *Brahma-parinama-vada*, however, is closer to the Munda philosophical tradition? Neither of these is true for Singbonga when He comes and resides in Nature. For, Singbonga merely resides in Nature and Nature itself does not become Singbonga. Nature becomes only a base, a place to sit and reside for Singbonga when Singbonga is invoked into the world by humans with the pahan performing the role of a *minister* (intermediary). Singbonga comes down to the *world*—His *creation*; on the invocation of the humans. He does not transform Himslef into the creation or the Nature, like the concept discussed in *Brahma-vivarta-vada* of Sankara or *Brahma-parinama-vada* of Ramanuja. But Nature is necessary for Singbonga to come down and relate to the people, accept worship, sacrifice and oblations. He does not reside in temples, churches or mosques. Singbonga can reside only in Nature. So when nature is destroyed, Sinbonga's place of residence on earth is destroyed and man gets more and more alienated from Singbonga. In this, Singbonga is not the loser, but man is. Because, Singbonga does not need the humans to exist, he can exist without them

However, Singbonga is also the keeper or maintainer of order in Nature, as indicated by *Asur Kani*. When Singbonga notices that there is disorder in the Nature due to incessant iron-smelting and the earth is getting heated up, he can destroy the culprits (as in *Asur Kani*) or He can bring about *rain of fire* (as in the legend of *Rain of Fire*).

Now, there is another question that can be put here: 'Is concept like *Brahma-vivarta-vada* or *Brahma-parinama-vada* possible?'

Creation in Vedic philosophy is not *ex nihilio*. The *Panchatatva* (five primordial elements) are eternal—they have never been created nor have ever been destroyed. It is out of these Panchatatva that creation comes into being, and the Eternal Being, the *Purusha* created itself into what we call many. Both *Purushasukta*[194] and Hymn of Creation[195] accept the pre-existence and eternality of *Panchatatva.* The *panchatatvas* are matter. Now, there is yet another which is Eternal, the Brahman or the Atman. The Brahman or the Atman, as per Katha Upnishad[196], is the Ultimate Reality. But Brahman or Atman is Pure Spirit or Pure Consciousness (*Sat, Chit Ananda*—Existence, Consciousness and Bliss). Has creation come out of this Brahman: *sat-chit-ananda*? Or the creation has sprung up on its own with the principle of Purusha, in accordance with the Purushasukta? Here itself two ultimate realities: the *sat-chit-ananda* (*Brahman* or *Atman*—which is *Pure Spirit or Pure Consciousness*) and the Panchatatva (five elements) are present. The concept of *Brahma-vivarta-vada* or *Brahma-parinama-vada* seems to run into a contradiction, here. How can Brahman or Atman (*Pure Spirit*) 'convert' or 'cause' itself into *Matter*—the world? If it can, Brahman or Atman should have some Panchatatva (*matter*) content in Him and hence for the very reason of carrying *Panchatatva* element in Him, Brahman or Atman is limited. Pure Spirit, going by hard logic, ought not to convert itself into matter.

In the Munda philosophy too, two Ultimate Realities—Spirit (Mind) and Matter are admitted: i) Singbonga, who is pure *Spirit* with the capability of carrying attributes as he can embody Himself in *matter*, and ii) the *matter* (the five original elements). Munda philosophy, in this way, is close to the *Dvaitavad* (Dualism), the Vedic concept defended by Madhava.

Madhava, who holds that God, soul and matter are eternal and absolutely real, though soul and matter is dependent on God,[197] is what the Munda philosophy holds too. Singbonga has the power to destroy the *soul,* or has the power to destroy the *matter.* The soul and the matter are dependent on Singbonga, as the Asur Kani would bear upon serious scrutiny. Even when Singbonga comes down on the invocation of the *pahan* to reside in Nature, He does not convert Himself into Nature. This too establishes Dualism—that spirit and matter, are two eternal entities and two ultimate realities, in Munda philosophy. The common belief *Brahma satya, Jagat mithya* does not hold ground with the Mundas. For the Mundas, both *Brahman is satya and Jagat too is.* Thus, *Brahma satya and Jagat satya*—as held by Dualism of Madhava in the Vedic tradition, is what Munda philosophy is similar to. On the other hand, a belief in *Brahma-vivarta-vada* or *Brahma-parinama-vada* concepts of Sankara and Ramanuja respectively, presupposes Supreme Spirit performing *ex-nihilo* creation, in which *spirit* can create *matter.* And this is the stand that is held by Christian philosophy too, though some are of the opposite view, stating the earth to be a formless void, darkness, waters and air were already existent when Yahweh God decided to create[198]. In this case, the word *'ex-nihilo'*, used usually for Christian story of *creation out of nothing,* is a creation of human mind actually out of nothing.

Omnipresent, Omnipotent and Omniscient

"Singbonga, the lord of them all is explicitly declared to be everywhere and seeing everything."[199] Singbonga is

Omnipresent, just like the Vedic Brahman or Atman, or Yahweh God of Christian philosophical tradition. He can reside in *sirma* and at the same time come down to earth and reside in the Nature (*sal* tree) when the *pahan* invokes Him. Sitting in the *sirma* (heaven), Singbonga can feel what afflictions and joys have been felt by the beings on earth. This is an attribute that Singbonga is blessed with, as part of His supreme might. Gods in Vedic as well as Christian philosophical traditions too, are blessed with supreme qualities like omniscience and omnipotence, apart from omnipresence. All these qualities can be found in Singbonga too, on analysis of Asur Kani and other legends. It is due to these qualities that men on earth worship Him and offer Him sacrifices.

Absoluteness

In philosophy, metaphysics, religion and spirituality, the term 'Absolute' is used for the 'most real being'. Absolute is conceived as 'being itself' or the being that transcends all other beings and comprehends them all. Vedic Brahman is an Absolute Being. 'The Absolute of the Upanishads manifests itself as the subject as well as the object, and transcends them both.'[200] The ultimate reality is Absolute, and transcends all, and pervades everything, point the Upanishads. The Christian God too, is Absolute and transcends all and pervades all. He is the ultimate reality from where springs the creation and to which everything returns.

But, is Singbonga Absolute, and does the Munda God fit the standard definition that the Vedic Brahman and

Christian God fit into? One has to go back to story of Creation and the *Asur Kani* in the Munda philosophy in order to analyse whether Singbonga is Absolute God. Both the legends validate that Singbonga is Creator God, Preserver God and Destroyer too. Just as the Veda's Brahman who can be all of these, and hence be Absolute, the Singbonga too is. Singbonga too is Creator, Preserver and Destroyer. He can create the spirits (tutelary spirits) and also preserve or destroy them. He creates the world and also preserves or destroys it. Thus, if Brahman is Absolute, Singbonga too is; for the two play similar roles and enjoy similar attributes and might. As for the Christian God, he has long been accepted as Absolute. As far as Absoluteness is concerned, Singbonga stands at equal footing with Christian God and Vedic God, the Brahman. The souls of good men after death go back to Singbonga and reside with Him in sirma (heaven), while those which could not live a good life, get rebirth as members in the same clan, as human beings. Souls of deliberate evil men (those are [illegible] evil in the Munda society) are punished by Singbonga and reduced to *evil spirits* which keep roaming for liberation or rebirth in this very world.

Bongas (tutelary spirits) and Vedic gods

Bonga is defined as 'any spirit conceived as wielding influence for good or evil over men and their affairs'[201]. Specifications are names of places in which the various spirits are supposed to have their abode.

Bongas are not gods, but the spirits who are generally benevolent, and in few cases malevolent. The benevolent spirits (bongas) are created by Singbonga Himself. In the Asur legend, when Singonga was going back to *sirma* (heaven) after destroying the Asurs who due to their greed and disobedience, incessant smelting of iron, had heated up the world. Upon realising that they have been ruined after the death of their husbands in the brick furnace, the Asur women clung on to Singbonga. They asked Him, 'How shall we live'? He told them, 'Had you cared to obey my commands not to heat up the world, all of you would have survived'. 'Now we have understood and we want to live by your commands. Make an arrangement for our life before you go back'. 'You will take care of the places where you fall, and the pahan will offer you sacrifice and food to live by'. Singbonga then shook Himself violently and in that act, the Asur women fell strewn all over the world. Some fell on the river, some on the paddy fields, some on the pebbles, some in the ravines, some in the hills and the like. The souls of these Asur women then became the *bongas* (spirits) and wherever the Asur women fell, their souls resided in those places and they came to be known the *keepers* of those places. The pahan of a village is supposed to know them by name, and offer them the required sacrifices. In return, these *bongas* take care of the places they resided in, and protect the people of the vicinity. All that the people of the place are required is to make regular sacrifice and food offerings to them through the *pahan* of the village. These souls of Asur women are benevolent spirits, for they had repented their evil acts and decided to live by the command of Singbonga. The malevolent spirits are those souls of the men who die after having lived a bad life and so Singbonga does not allow them inside *sirma*. Neither do they take rebirth. They keep roaming about, disturbed and tormented, trying to harm people as per their habit. But the evil spirits can be restricted from doing so by a person called *deora* (sort of witch-finder) who can detect the identity of an evil spirit and keep it at a bay through institutions and invocation of Singbonga.

Some popular benevolent *bongas* are: *burubonga* (bonga of the hill), *ikirbonga* (bonga of the river or rivulet), *oraa-bonga (bonga* of the house, usually the *umbul* of the ancestors residing in a corner of the house), *baram-bonga* (lord on the earth second to Singbonga). These bongas usually reside in the natural objects and protect them.

In Vedic tradition too, one finds natural phenomena or objects deified. Rigveda is full of hymns in praise of such deities (gods). In later developments, these deities became prominent. Indra began as a god of lightning, thunder, storm, rains and river flows; only to later become a very powerful god and ruler of heaven. Agni is a very powerful god attributed to be the reigning deity in fire. Usha, Varuna et al, are gods who have their abode in nature.

There appears a huge similarity in the tradition of *bonga-making* in Munda philosophy and deifying nature and natural objects in Vedic philosophy. Till very recently before modern education came among the Munda race, bongas were extensively worshipped and offered sacrifices, just as the Vedic gods in Hindu religious tradition continue to wield power among believers. Whether the angels of Christian tradition can be compared and discussed with *bongas* of Munda tradition is a question. Angels are not reigning deities of nature and natural objects—as in the case of *bongas* and deities of nature or natural phenomena in Vedic tradition. But they can provide protective care to people who may call for them.

Man

The nature and stature of a man is similar to the nature and stature of the god he worships. If a man worships a god or deity who celebrates war and killing, the man would be exactly that. If a man worships a god who signifies love and forgiveness, he would be exactly that. And if a man worships a god who lays so much emphasis in fellow-feeling and community life, the man would value these as the command of god and live by them. Man is the product of the philosophy he adheres to and lives by. The lay allege that philosophy does not even bake a cake. Their poor intellect does not help them to see that philosophy finds that baking a cake is too mundane a job left to science and food technology, but it instead decides what meaning a man would live by in this world eating the cake baked by science, with what religious belief, with what social practices, with what rites and rituals, and with what worldview. What philosophy can do to society, someone has to come to India to see for himself, or for that matter, go to any country in the world where philosophy rules the roost. From birth to death, even after death, things that a man should believe in, do and live by; are decided by the Vedic philosophy. Thus, man basically is the product of the philosophy he chooses.

Munda philosophy generates a particular kind of 'man' who would be distinctively different from a 'man' generated by Vedic philosophy or Christian philosophy. A child is born as a *tabula rasa*, and it is this philosophy that writes god, values, ethos, beliefs, practices and worldview in his *tabula rasa* mind. A human civilisation, thus, basically is the stage or phase at which a 'mind' functions and interacts. If the 'mind' functions at a sophisticated stage, not caring to take gods, worldview, ethos and practices at their surface value, ever wanting to put them to empirical test, it is the civilisation that values empirically verified knowledge. All education systems and educational pedagogy are centred on 'moulding' this 'mind' in accordance with a philosophy that the author of the pedagogy may want to propagate.

A 'Munda man' will be what the Munda philosophy propagates with regard to social life, moral values, ethical standards, god, women-men, human relations, sexuality etc. He would be similar to the ethos and values that Singbonga holds. Even if some Mundas, whose forefathers once followed their ancestors' religious practice, have converted to Christianity, the residual of Munda philosophy in them is still very large. In fact, it will remain as a Munda Christian will always remain a man with Munda philosophy, and the chance that he will ever become like a 'European Christian', is bleak.

The Munda philosophy, particularly the *Story of Creation* and *Asur Kani*, has to be analysed closely in order to understand the Munda 'man'. Man is the highest creature among the animate and inanimate beings created by Singbonga. Nature is given to man in order to live with and take care of, because man has the intellect which is superior to other animate beings. Things like land and forest, does not become individual property, they become community property and a Munda man has to just till the land he inherits from his ancestors to draw his food (sustenance), take care of it by keeping it intact, and pass it on to the future generation as he had received it. Munda *man* is not the *master* of the land he tills, he is not the Master of Creation, as in the case of Christian philosophy. The British principle of 'Eminent Domain of the Crown' (which draws its origin from the Genesis of the Bible), under which all the land of the Domain ruled over by the Crown is the property of the Crown, cannot philosophically apply in the land of the Mundas.

The Biblical story of Creation places the Creation at the foot of *man* in order to lord over it, use it as per his will. Yahweh God appoints man as the master of all other beings, animate and inanimate, of the earth. A Munda man has to be Singbonga-like in nature. And as Singbonga is caring and providing to all, a Munda man has to be caring and providing to all. Man has to play the role of a *caretaker* of all the beings in creation, not its destroyer. When he tries to destroy or creates a situation to destroy the creation and created beings, Singbonga will bring about his destruction, as it happened in *Asur Kani*. In fact, as a natural law, destruction naturally follows when man tries to use the nature for his greed.

Man has to keep greed at bay. This was what is brought out by Asur Kani, the Legend of the Asurs. If he works to fulfil his greed, it will create disorder in the world (on earth) and animate and inanimate beings would be greatly disturbed. Singbonga sends messengers (symbols) to inform man that his act driven by greed is not for the order of the world, and he should mend his ways. If man does not heed to this message, eventual destruction is the only alternative. In the Asur Kani, Singbonga comes down to the earth and destroys the Asur who did not stop heating up the earth with their incessant iron-smelting.

Day and night were made by Singbonga so that man works during the day and rests by night. He should not work round-the-clock, for that does harm to man himself. Every Munda man should sing and dance (*susun-durang*) together as a community, in order to relax and live in a community. This is why songs and dance come natural to the Mundas. It has famously been said. *sen gi susun, kaji gi durang*— 'walking is like dancing, talking is like singing', about the Mundas.

Man and Woman are created at the same time, from the same stuff, unlike in Christianity where the Woman is created with the bones of Man, after the Man. Even in Vedic philosophy, *Viraj* (Self) begets the woman, because he was alone and he wanted to be two. 'He desired a mate. He became the size of a man and a wife in close embrace. He divided this body into two. From that division arose husband (pati) and wife (patni). He united with her. From that [union] human beings were born.'[202] 'How can he unite with me after having produced me from himself? Well, let me hide myself.''[203]

The passage uses Viraj in the sense of *man*. Man is the *Viraj*, man is *Self*, man is *pati*. Woman is born from this man *(pati)*. Man in Vedic philosophy has the pre-eminence in everything and is equal to *Self* or *Viraj*. Similar is the position held by Christian philosophy in the story of Creation. Munda philosophy differs from both the Vedic and Christian philosophy on man-woman relations, as man and woman were created together at the same time by Singbonga. Man is not pre-eminent as compared with woman in Munda philosophy.

In Munda philosophy, sacred work that a man should aspire to do is that which is aimed at the good of the larger Munda society. To live an anti-social life and practise individualism are sins. A man has to observe all those festivals that have been set by Singbonga, the Creator God. Festivals include Mage, Sarhul and Ba—occasions when Singbonga comes down to the earth and resides in the *shorea robusta* tree in a special way. Man should not destroy the creation, trees and herbs. He should instead take care of them.

Man, according to Munda philosophy, is essentially good, but his greed for riches and power may turn him evil. This is brought out by the Asur Kani. Greed and lust for power are two things that can blind a man. In the Asur Kani these were the two things that blinded the Asur men and they thought they should produce more iron and become richer and more powerful. They did not care for what their act was going to cause to the creation, the animate and inanimate beings in the creation. In the Asur Legend, Singbonga sends many messengers to the Asurs, but they fail to convince them. Instead, they are chased away after being insulted. Man does not want to sacrifice his own progeny, but he is ever willing to find a victim in other community for the sacrifice. Thus, man holds that sacrificing to God or deity–particularly when it comes to human sacrifice is 'bad' as long as the victim is one of his kin, and when the victim could be anybody, even outside the clan, then even this 'bad' becomes 'not objected'. Thus, what is 'good' and what is 'bad' is not always decided by man's rationality—this issue is decided by who is involved, my own kin or someone else, as derived from the Asur Kani.

Sexuality

A man in Munda philosophy has to live his life with a woman, have sex and produce children to further human race. As per the story of procreation of the Mundas, boy and girl live side by side without knowing what sex is. Singbonga himself has to come to officiate their union ceremony (marriage), at which rice beer is prepared and used. Thus going strictly by Munda philosophy, premarital sex is an alien concept in Munda society, and is regarded unethical and immoral. However, modernity has changed the way today's Munda looks at premarital consensual sex. Women, however, are not seen as sex objects meant only to play the second fiddle to man. Woman is a companion with equal human rights as the man, with gender equality. Living a single life without marriage is not regarded 'good' in the Munda society. Taking a woman as wife is a must, according to the rules set by Singbonga Himself.

Relation of sexes is different in different societies, and has its base on the philosophy of a particular society. In Munda society, sexes relate to each other on equal terms; man is not superior to woman, neither is woman inferior to man. Though Munda society is not male chauvanistic, the generation runs on the *male line* (patriarchal), which is probably because of the society's adherence to a male god, Singbonga.

In Christian philosophy, woman is created only after the man. So, relation of sexes in Christian philosophy is tilted towards man, though secular western philosophy, through reasons, may not accept this position. Similar is the situation in Vedic philosophy where purusha (*Viraj* or *Self*) is more 'male-centric', than 'female-centric'; in that He becomes the size of two, and 'the *he* (man) unites with her' (woman)[204]. The *man*, in fact, is equal to *God* Himself.

Soul

The Atman of the Veda and the two-layered *jiu* or *ji* or *jiyom* (soul) of the Munda philosophy and the initial '*life breath*' of the Abrahamic tradition in recent days being known as *'soul'* in Christian philosophy, requires a detail discussion. Soul is that which survives the body after the death of a person.

Jiu or *ji* (the Munda soul) has two-layers in it. While the second layer is *roa* and the primary layer is known as *'umbul'* or *'longoy'*; and both collectively make *ji* or *jiu*. When a *jiu* is embodied in a man, the body also gets an umbul (shade), which becomes part and parcel of the *jiu*. While *jiu* survives death and is eternal, roa and umbul too survive after the death of a person, but get separated soon after. During the dream, it is *roa*, not the *umbul*, which leaves the body and wanders about: it is not good to wake up people abruptly without leaving the roa time to re-enter the body.

Munda philosophy believes that *ji* further, is the principle of life found not only in men, but also in animals and plants. In plants, however, it has only the vegetative power, in animals moreover it has faculty of sensuous perception and the appetitive and locomotive faculties; in man, in addition to all these, it has reason and rational appetitive or will. *Jiu* does not have layers in animal and vegetation, and when a plant or animal dies, its *ji* dwindles into the air, i.e., it disappears, it is annihilated. The *ji* of a man is immortal, and when the person dies, its *roa* layer goes to the *'bitarpur'*, the inner dwelling, also called *'porom disom'*, the country beyond (the next world) there to receive from Singbonga a reward or punishment.

The *ji (roa* and *umbul* collectively) being the 'principle of life'[205], cannot leave the body without causing death, except for a very short while during a swoon or collapse; if it comes back at once, life will not be lost and the man will revive and live again. The *roa* is not bound to remain continually in the body during life. Nearly every night when the body lies down to sleep and the *umbul* remains with the body, and *roa* is off for an outing. *Roa* sees and hears when it thus wanders around, meeting people and situations. Nevertheless, it should not remain absent for too long. A few hours can do no harm. But, if the roa remains absent from the body for weeks; the *umbul* of the body may no longer be able to keep the body alive.

The Mundas have a whole theory of genesis and interpretation of dreams. The roa is not bound to remain continually in the body during life though its continued absence would in the long run prove equally fatal. What we call dreams is just what our *roa* sees and hears on these trips.

Often, if not always, *roa* then sees things not as actually they are in progress but as they are going to happen shortly.

According to Munda philosophy, when roa is free of the body, it is gifted with a *'prophetic insight'* into the near future. It may moreover either see the actors of these events in their unveiled reality, just as they are or it may see then as symbolic appearance. An individual man is nearly always seen by the wandering roa under the shape of such animal as he resembles by character or, at least, a man stands for an animal, and vice versa.

Thus, if in a dream one sees a person die, it means that either he is going to kill some game in the chase of that he is going to lose one of his domestic animals. "If he dreams of a dying animal he must expect the demise of a member of his own household, a co-villager or other relation. If he dreams that an animal enters his house he knows that he will soon have a visitor or guest. If he meets a man in his dream he will in reality come across an animal. A snake indicates a quiet but successful man, an elephant a quiet but fearless one".[206]

The *umbul* (shade) on the other hand, is the part of the ji which remains forever in the house of his descendants after the death of the physical body, and the Mundas have a ceremony to invite the *umbul* back into the house. *Umbul* (shade) is not the ji (soul), but the outer part that the roa of the soul parts with when it leaves the body. When the person dies and the umbul gets separated from *roa*, *roa* alone becomes the complete *jiu* in the absence of a body, either ready to move to *sirma* or get embodied again. If it gets embodied again and takes rebirth, it gets a new body and also a new *umbul*.

On the death of a person when roa moves away from the body as a complete *jiu*, leaving the *umbul* behind, the family members assign a corner of the house for this *umbul*, where the *umbul* (shade) of the person lives and protects the members from all evil.

Rebirth is only for the *ji* (soul) of a person who fails to live a noble life. The *ji* may take a rebirth, usually in the family itself or in the same clan, as a human being. If a child is born soon after the death of an elderly person, the child would be named after the dead. It is believed that the grandfather's soul is again born in the same house as the grandson. However, the new child's body acquires a new *umbul* (shade), and the *umbul* of the grandfather would be assigned a corner to live in. Noble living, according to Munda worldview, is living an upright and moral life, prescribed by the Munda society, a harmonious and loving life with other people in society, without hatred, jealousy, greed or ill-will.

Thus, the concept of *karma*, as defined in the Vedas, is found in Munda philosophy to a degree. There is a belief that if someone is evil by action, he is punished by Singbonga and he usually meets an unnatural death, and his *ji* keeps wandering about all through. His *umbul* (shade) too is not invited back into the house. There is no *rebirth* for such a 'soul' and the soul becomes an evil spirit. A *ji*, which tried to live a noble life but could not do so due to some reason or the other, gets a rebirth as another chance to get itself rewarded a place by Singbonga in *sirma*.

Unlike Vedic philosophy that has elaborately developed the concept of soul (*Atman*), the concept of soul (*Ji*) in

Munda philosophy has not been well developed, and it remains mostly simple. Munda philosophy, however, is a staunch believer in the philosophical position of eternality of *Ji*. It is believed that *Ji* came to the man and the woman from the *Eternal Ji* (Singbonga) Himself when He created their idols and set a portion of His own *Ji* in each of them. So when the embryo gets life, Singbonga puts in it a portion of His own *Ji*, and it becomes the *life principle* of the child. It is due to this reason that abortion is seen as killing a *Ji* in the Munda philosophy and not recommended. Anyone doing so is seen as killing a *Ji*.

Microcosm and and Macrocosm

The individual Self (Atman) of the Vedic philosophy is blended with the microcosm and the macrocosm. So is the case even for soul (*Ji*) of the Munda philosophy. But while the macrocosm *Atman* has three initial states: *waking, dreaming and sound sleep*, and the Fourth is the *Jagrat*—the Brahman. The *Ji* layers: *roa* and *umbul*, both of which collectively make the *Ji* in a living man. The roa can be transcendent, but *umbul* has to live on the earth alone, usually in the corner of the house where family members assign it a place. The *Atman* of Vedic tradition and the *Roa* of Munda tradition thus have similarity to some extent, as far as their eternality and transcendentalism is concerned.

While Christian philosophy grapples to establish the concept of 'soul', Munda philosophy has a rich concept of 'soul'. The Atman of the Vedic tradition is probably the richest in the philosophical traditions, but the *Ji* of Munda tradition is no dwarf. *Ji* is as Divine and Eternal as the Atman of the Vedic tradition. That concept of Creation gets well-explained and expounded by Munda Philosophy, what the Munda Philosophy scores over other philosophies is with regard to ecological destruction and its eventual consequence. The Philosophy prophesies what is going to come if humans follow their lust for riches and power by heating up the earth in the process of incessant production, be it industrial or mining. This philosophical prophesy is far more far-sighted than even Vedic and Christian philosophies. Propagation of this point in Munda philosophy in the right spirit and inculcation in the worldview of the people in general may eventually prove greatly helpful in addressing the issue of global warming and the danger of destruction of earth that lurks today.

Munda Philosophy manages to explain the problem of soul, eternality of soul, rebirth, reward and punishment of the souls. Interstingly, the Munda concept of soul is able to explain dream, and why a man does not die when he is asleep and his soul moves around meeting people, animals and things—what we usually call 'dream'. Other philosophies leave this dream phenomenon to psychology for an explanation, but the Munda philosophy throws light on it. In fact, the Munda race has an extensive dream analysis that people have observed and recorded over the years of sharing dreams and their consequences with each other.

Munda philosophy also manages to explain modern issues of gender equality, sexuality, abortion etc. These issues can be discussed elaborately with Munda philosophy as the 'base', just like other established philosophies, including Vedic and

Christian—the two great philosophies of the world. Munda philosophy also explains philosophically, just as the Vedic and Christian philosophies do, matters of Creation and Primordial stuff. Another important philosophical issue: Dualism (*Dvaita*) or Non-Dualism (*Advaita*) of the Vedas, the two concepts that engaged best philosophical brains ever born in India, too, can be discussed in the context of Munda philosophy. Christian and western philosophy's problem of '*body and spirit*' (*mind-body* relations), too, can be discussed in/with Munda philosophy. As discussed earlier, Mundas are akin to *Dvaita-vada*, in that they hold both spirit and matter as two ultimate realities, able to interact with one another at a level that mysticism can better explain than logic. The pre-existence of primordial elements have been admitted right at the outset in the story of Creation. It is the spirit (Singbonga) that tries to create animated beings using the primordial elements and His own Spirit.

Equality of sexes is what Munda philosophy stands out on. In fact, this philosophy is lived by the people of the race. Boy and girl children are not differentiated on the basis of sex, and are treated equally by parents. Women partake in all the social functions; but some religious functions are wholly male-domianted, particularly those that involve a *pahan*. *Pahan* has to be a male, and the Munda race has not yet opened the position to females.

The Vedas are the source of origin of varnas in Hinduism. The Munda philosophy accepts the eternity of *pahanship* as an institution, from the beginning of human creation. The first man was the first *pahan* who worshipped

Singbonga after Singbonga created him and the woman along with him. He was ordered by Sinbonga to worship and offer him sacrifices, and the man did. Hence, *pahan* has to be from the first line of the generation, in the sense that he has to be the first born son of the first born son of the first born son who establishes the village he lives in as his other men and women do.[207] Thus, *pahan-ship* was instituted by Singbonga God himself. The Vedas also talk of the origin of *rajan* (ruler) from the primordial man. Munda philosophy discusses the orgin of *ruler* in the Munda race in a different way. Initially, the posts of *pahan* and rajan (*priest* and *ruler*) lay in the person who established a village. But, the concept of *rulership* happened as part of social evolution, not as part of philosophical evolution, as in the case of pahanship. A legend earlier mentioned discusses how the younger brother who was physically stronger, was assigned the post of 'ruler' (*Munda*) by the father and how the elder brother, who was physically less strong kept the role of *pahanship* with him. The head of the village or region who had the authority to rule over the people, is known as Munda in the Munda race. Thus, the word 'Munda' has a third meaning too. It means 'head', the ruler.

Some scholars, especially those who have not a trace of understanding of the Munda group or Munda philosophy, have in recent days been trying to place them under a category of the Vedic tradition. Such attempts are not easy as Mundas have been rulers in their own right for several centuries, or for that matter many other tribal groups across the country too have been rulers.

Vedic tradition and Munda tradition have lived side by side and have evolved side by side in India. There are some similarities between the two but there are also some differences. In the due course of living side by side, one must have influenced the other. Which philosophy has received what, to which degree and from whom, is a subject of study. Simplistic observation would not do justice to the subject, each of Vedic and Munda traditions claims that the other has taken a lot from its own. Famous scholar Suniti Kumar Chatterjee, in his book "Bharatiya Arya Bhasa Aur Hindi", is of the view that many concepts, beliefs and practices have been adopted by the Vedic tradition from the Munda tradition[208] and that many temples had been begun by the Munda *pahans* initially. Chatterjee says that things like Ganga as sacred river, vermilion on the forehead of a married woman; trees, rocks, stones, rivers as deities, orgin of *Aryan gotra* system from *totem system* of Mundas etc. have been adopted from Austro-Asiatic (Munda) race[209].

On the other hand, there has indeed been Hinduisation of sections of the Munda race—just as Chritianisation of another—and terms like *Thakur* (*Thakur Jiu*), now used by Santals is a clear Hindu import.

Unlike the Vedic Philosophy and Christian Philosophy, why has Munda Philisophy been not yet brought in written form? This is a question the answer of which should be given by each knowledge-loving educated individual irrespective of race or creed.

Even the Vedic Philosophy remained a *sruti* for a long time, for millennia. Vedas were known by heart by a section of the Brahmins in India, carefully preserved in mind and passed to the next generation. When the British came and they came to know of the Vedas, they started looking for books. They realised that the Vedas are completely in the mind (*sruti*) of the Brahmins. We have today written Vedas, though they are still regarded as *sruti*. This did not happen for Munda philosophy. Though British and the Western scholars documented Munda knowledge, culture, art, practice, language etc, for Munda philosophy *per se*, the task to bring it into written form just as the Vedas or Christian philosophies, is still awaited. However, many records of the British and the western scholars—16 Volume Encyclopaedia Mundarica being an example—include philosophical components of the Austro-Asiatic Munda race in bits and pieces, in written form. A written body of knowledge ensures completeness and preservation for itself. Searching minds willing to study Munda philosophy can have ready access to it for further discussion and deliberation. It only exposes the Munda Philosophy for further evolution, which is necessary for human knowledge to progress.

❑

End Notes

Chapter 1

[1]Narrated by Raju Kerketta, Maruianus Kerketta, Shilvanus Budh, Gautam Lakra and Biju Nayak, who reside in Panchora-Koilsar, a forest-village bordering Jharkhand-Odisha. The five collectively are famously known in the region as *Hathi Kheda* group for the last ten year and can understand the language of the elephants. Man-animal conflicnt in this region is acute and the group is highly sought-after for intervention. As claimed by them, even the elephants in the region understand their language and obey them.

[2] J.B. Foffman, the Roman Catholic missionary who authored Encyclopaedia Mundarica in 16 Volumes, refers to Asur Kani in these words.

[3] Hoffman, *Encyclopaedia Mundarica*, 1648-1658.

[4] Ibid

[5] Sharma, *Problems of Philosophy*, 197.

[6] Vatsyayan, *History of Western Philosophy*, 91.

[7] The New Jerusalem Bible, Book of Genesis, Verse- 1:28-29.

Chapter 2

[8]Story partly contributed by Dr Sumit Kerketta, a resident of Koronjo near Bombokera in Simdega district of Jharkhand. Jharkhand is a principal homeland of Munda tribes in India.

[9]*Tabula rasa* (blank slate) is a theory propounded by philosopher John Locke which says that individuals are born without built in mental content and that therefore all knowledge comes from experience or sense perception.

[10]Trigunayat, 17.

[11]Roy, *The Mundas and Their Country*, 59 ff.

[12]Van Exem, *The Religious System of the Munda Tribe*, 12.

[13]Ibid

[14]Roy, *The Mundas and Their Country*, 1.

[15]Staal, *Discovering the Vedas*, 23.

[16]Roy, *Mundas and Their Country*, p. 1.

[17]*Mahabharata*, *Bhisma-Badha Parva*, 117, 23.

[18]Kumar, *Jharkhand Me Mundaon ka Arthik Etihas*, 49.

[19]*Kesri, Chotanagpur ka Eitihas*, 9.

[20]*Roy, Mundas and Their Country*, 23.

[21]*Kumar, Jharkhand Me Mundaon ka Arthik Etihas*, 32.

[22]Roy, *Mundas and Their Country* 49; and Kumar, *Jharkhand Me Mundaon ka Arthik Etihas*, 45.

[23]Roy, *Mundas and Their Country*, 36; and Kumar, *Jharkhand Me Mundaon ka Arthik Etihas*, 53.

[24]Roy, *Mundas and Their Country*, p 36.

[25]Ibid

[26]Kumar, *Jharkhand Me Mundaon ka Arthik Etihas*, 25.

[27]Roy, *Mundas and Their Country*, 50.

[28]Ibid, 22.

[29]Rigveda, II, 14, 6.

[30]Rigveda, I, 53, 9.

[31]Rigveda, I, 174, 8.

[32]Roy, *Mundas and Their Country*, 36.

[33]Kumar, *Mundaok ka Arthik Itihas*, 53.

[34]Hoffman, *Enyclopaedia Mundarica*, 1763.

[35]Kesri, *Chotanagpur Ka Itihas*, 7.

[36]Hoffman, *Enyclopaedia Mundarica*, 1764.

[37]Oral history in narration among the Kharias of Chotanagpur.

[38]Kesri, *Chotanagpur ka Itihas*, 10.

[39]Sharma, *A Critical survey of Indian Philosophy*, 13.

[40]Hoffman, *Encyclopaedia Mundarica*, 3973.

CHAPTER 3

[41]Roy, *Mundas and Their Country*, 7.

[42]Hoffman, *Enclypadia Mundarica*, Vol. VI, 1648-1658.

[43]Elwin, *Agaria*, 154.

[44]Ibid.

[45]Kumar, *Jharkhand Me Munda ka Arthik Itihas*, 52.

[46]Hoffman, *Encyclopaedia Mundarica*, Vol. XIII, 3819.

[47]Rev. Stephen Murmu, a professor of Christian Theology and Ethics at Santal Theological College, Benagaria, in his paper *'Understanding the Concept of God in Santal Traditional Myth'* quotes George E. Somerse, The Dynamics of Santal Tradition in a Peasant Society p. 38.

[48]Rev. Stephen Murmu, a professor of Christian Theology and Ethics at Santal Theological College, Benagaria, in his

paper *'Understanding the Concept of God in Santal Traditional Myth'*, published in *Indian Journal of Theology*, published by Bishops College, Kolkata, p. 74.

[49]Murmu, *Understanding the Concept of God in Santal Traditional Myth*, 75.

[50]Sinha, *Santhal Hul*, 33.

[51]Sinha, *Santhal Hul*, 33.

[52]Murmu, *Understanding the Concept of God in Santal Traditional Myth*, 75.

[53]Murmu, p. 74.

[54]Bodding, *Studies in Santhal Medicine and Folklore*, 1.

[55]Hoffman, *Encyclopaedia Mundarica*, Vol. XIII, 3874.

[56]Ibid, Vol. VIII, 2333.

[57]ibid

[57]Dungdung, *Kharia Jeewan aur Paramparae*, 27-28.

[59]Ibid, 192-193.

[60]Kerketta, *Kharia Lok Kathao ka Sahityik aur Sanskritik Adhyayan*, 91.

[61]Hoffman, *Encyclopaedia Mundarica*, Vol. VI, 1763.

[62]Ibid, Vol. VI, 1764.

[63]Ibid, Vol. VI, 1765.

[64]Hoffman, *Encyclopaedia Mundarica*, Vol. VI, 1765.

[65]Ibid, Vol. VI, p. 1769.

[66]Sinha, Aditya Prasad, Ho Lok Katha, 45-50

[67]Hoffman, *Encyclopaedia Mundarica*, Vol. XIII, p. 3973.

[68]Ibid, Vol. II, 324.

[69]Ibid, Vil. II, 424.

[70]Munda, *Adi Dharam*, 12; and Dungdung, *Kharia lok Kathaon ka Sahityik aur Sanskritik Adhyayan*, 73

Chapter 4

[71]Sharma, *A Critical Survey of Indian Philosophy*, 18

[72]Swami Nikhilananda, *The Upanishads*, 13.

[73]Staal, *Discovering the Vedas*, xvi.

[74]Ibid, 4.

[75]Ibid.

[76]Ibid.

[77]Roy, *Mundas and Their Country*, 32; Rigveda I, 130, 8; Rigveda 8, 104, 2; Rigveda 5, 45, 6.

[78]Staal, *Discovering the Vedas*, 23.

[79]Ibid

[80]Staal, *Discovering the Vedas*, 54.

[81]Staal, *Discovering the Vedas*, 73.

[82]Ibid, 14.

[83]Rigveda, 7.26.1.

[84]Staal, *Discovering the Vedas*, 18.

[85]Rigveda 10. 090 (English Translation, RTH Griffit).

[86]Swami Nikhilananda, *The Upanishads*, 2.

[87]Ibid, 215.

[88]Rig Veda, 10.37.

[89]Ibid, 10.37.4.

[90]Ibid, 1.91.1-2.

[91]Rig Veda, 1.91.23.

[92]Rig Veda, 1.179.

[93]Elwin, *Agaria* 18-19.

[94]Elwin, *Agaria*, 155.

[95]Elwin, *Agaria*, 159.

[96]Published by Deep Publication, New Delhi, 2009.

[97]Staal, *Discovering the Vedas*, 136.

[98]Ibid.

[99]Ibid, 138.

[100]Ibid, 139.

[101]Ibid.

[102]Editorial page of the book published by Gokul Bhawan, K 37/109, Gopal Mandir Lane, Varanasi, 2009.

[103]Staal, *Discovering the Vedas*, 103.

[104]Sharma, *A Critical Survey of Indian Philosophy*, 16.

[105]Rig Veda, 10.164.46.

[106]Sharma, *A Critical Survey of Indian Philosophy*, 16.

[107]Ibid.

[108]Staal, *Discovering the Vedas*, xvi.

[109]Sharma, *A Critical Survey of Indian Philosophy*, 24.

[110]Ibid, 346.

[111]Ibid.

[112]Sharma, *A Critical Survey of Indian Philosophy*, 373.

[113]Ibid.

Chapter 5

[114]Hoffman, *Encyclopaedia Mundarica*, Vol. VII, 2056.

[115]Ibid, Vol. II, p. 501

[116]Ibid, Vol. II, p. 501.

[117]Ibid, Vol. XII, p. 3619.

[118]Hoffman, *Encyclopaedia Mundarica*, Vol. VIII, p. 2524.

[119]iMunda, *Adi Dharam*, 35.

[120]Murmu, *'Understanding the Concept of God in Santal Traditional Myth'*, 79.

[121]Ibid, p. 84.

[122]Kerketta, *Kharia Lok Kathao ka Sahityik aur Sanskritik Adhyayan*, 24.

[123]Rig Veda, 10. 90.

[124]Katha Upanishad, 1.iii.3.

[125]Sharma, *A Critical Survey of Indian Philosophy*, 24-25.

[126]Mundaka Upanishad, II.i.5.

[127]Prasna Upanishad, 1.13.

[128]Aitareya Upanishad, 2. i.1.

[129]Ibid, 2.i.2.

[130]Brihadaranyaka Upanishad, 1.iv.3.

[131]Ibid, 6.ii.13.

[132]Brihadaranyaka Upanishad, 6.iv.2.

[133]Ibid 6.iv.3.

[134]Trigunayat, Munda Lok Kathayen, 35.

[135]Ibid 34-35.

[136]Father Pierre Du Jarric, *Akbar and The Jesuits: An Account of the Jesuit Mission to the Court of Akbar*, 18.

[137]Ibid, xxxix.

[138]Ibid, 1.

[139]Ibid. 8.

[140]Ibid, 9.

[141]Ibid, 4.

[142]Ibid, 16.

[143]Ibid, 29.

[144]Ibid, 30.

[145]Ibid, 20.

[146]Ibid.

[147]Ibid, 30.

[148]Ibid, 84.

[149]Ibid, viii.

[150]Oraons are a close neighbour of the Mundas in Central India. Though linguistically the two groups are different, they have been sharing, in recent days, a common past.

Their supreme god is known as *Dharme.* They belong to the Dravidian linguistic family.

[151]Clarysse, L: *Father Constant Lievens*, 110.

[152]Ibid, p. 111.

[153]Ibid.

[154]The Bible, Gensis, 2.23.

[155]Psalms, 8. 3-6.

[156]Job, 7. 17.

[157]The New Testament, First Letter to Tmothy, 1. 17.

[158]Ibid, 6.16.

[159]The Bible, Letter to the Hebrew, 9. 27.

[160]The Bible, Genesis, 2.20-23.

[161]The Bible, Genesis 1.1b.

[162]The Bible, Genesis, 1.1c.

[163]Ibid 1.10.

[164]Ibid 1.26.

[165]The Bible, Genesis, 3.5.

[166]The Bible, Genesis, 1.26.

[167]Ibid, 2.23.

[168]Ibid, 2.24.

[169]The Bible, Genesis, 3.2-3.

[170]Ibid 3.7.

[171]Ibid 3.8.

[172]Ibd 4.1

[173]The Bible, Gensis, 2. 7.

[174]Ibid, 4.1.

[175]Ibid, 4. 8.

[176]The Bible, Gospel of Mathew, 2.20.

[177]The Bible, Book of Acts, 2.41.

[178]Caird and Hurst, *New Testament Theology*, 267.

[179]Ford and Muers, *The Modern Theologians: Introduction to Christian Theology*, 693.

[180]The Bible, Gospel of Mathew, 10.28.

[181]The Bible, Gosel of St Luke, 9.25.

[182]Vatsyayan, *History of Western Philosophy*, 30.

[183]Ibid.

[184]Ibid, 31.

[185]Ibid.

[186]Ibid, 51.

[187]Ibid. 56.

[188]Ibid.

[189]Bhagavat Gita, 2.20.

CHAPTER 6

[190]Munda, *Adi Dharam*, 14.

[191]Swami Nikhilananda, *The Upanishads*, 17.

[192]Hoffman, *Encyclopaedia Mundarica*, Vol. I, p. 242.

[193]Munda, *Adi Dharam*, 12-13.

[194]Rigveda, 10.90.

[195]Rigveda, 10.129.

[196]*Katha Upanishad*, 2. 3-4 and Sharma, *A Critical Survey of Indian Philosophy*, 23.

[197]Sharma, *A Critical Survey of Indian Philosophy*, 373.

[198]The Jerusalem Bible, Geneis 1 footnote b. p, 1.

[199]Hoffman, *Encyclopaedia Mundarica*, Vol. II, 614.

[200]Sharma, *A Critical Survey of Indian Philosophy*, 25.

[201]Hoffman, *Encyclopaedia Mundarica, Vol. II*, p. 612.

[202]*Brihadaranyaka Upanishad*, 1.iv.3.

[203]Ibid, 1.iv.4.

[204]*Brihadaranyaka Upanishad*, 1.iv.3.

[205]Hoffman, *Encyclopaedia Mundarica*, Vol. VII, 2053.

[206]Ibid, Vol. VIII, p. 2524.

[207]Ibid, Vol. XI, p. 3210.

[208]Trigunayat, *Munda Lok-Kathayen*, 35.

[209]Ibid, 36.

Bibliography

- Batayal, Rakesh: *The Penguin Book of Modern Indian Speeches*, Penguin Books, New Delhi, 2007.
- Caird, G.B. & Hurst, L.D.: *New Testament Theology*, Oxford University Press, UK, 1994.
- Clarysse, L: *Father Constant Lievens*, Satya Bharti, Ranhi, 1985.
- Dungdung, Joakim: *Kharia Jivan aur Parampara*, Ranchi Jesu Samaj, Ranchi, 1999.
- Elwin, Verrier: Agaria (Hindi translation), Rajkamal Prakashan, New Delhi, 2007.
- Father Du Jarric, Pierre: *Akbar and The Jesuits: An Account of the Jesuit Mission* to the Court of Akbar, Harper and Brother, New York and London, (date na).
- Ford, David F. (Ed.) with Muer, Rachel: *The Modern Theologians—An Introduction to Christian Theology*, Blackwell Publishing, UK, 2005.

- Hembrom, Ramesh: *Santali Lok Geet aur Jiwan Darshan*, Janmadhyam, Ranchi, 2012.
- J.B. Hoffman, J.B.: *Encyclopedia Mundarica*--16 Volumes, Gian Publishing House, New Delhi, Reprint 2009.
- Kerketta, Rose: *Kharia Lok-kathaye*, Annapurna Prakashan, Kanpur, 1990.
- Kesri, B.P: *Chhotanagpur ka Itihas*, Nagpuri Sansthan, Ranchi, 2009.
- Kumar, Anil: *Jharkhand Me Munda ka Arthik Itihas*, Janki Prakashan, Patna, 2002.
- Mahato, Shailendra: *Jharkhand Ki Samargatha*, Danish Books, New Delhi, 2015.
- Munda, Ram Dayal: *Adi Dharam*, Rajkamal Prakashan, New Delhi, 2009
- Munda, Ram Dayal: *Seled*, Sael Rakab Puthi Centre, Kolkata, 2005.
- Murmu, Stephen: *Understanding the Concept of God in Santhal Traditiuonal Myths* in Indian Journal of Theology, Bishop's College, Kolkata, date n.a.
- Nikhilananda, Swami: *The Upanishads*, Advaita Ashram, Kolkata, 2012.
- Roy, S.C: *The Mundas and their Country*, Man In India, Ranchi, 1968 (Reprint).

- Sharma, Chandradhar: *A Critical Survey of Indian Philosophy*, Motilal Banarasidass Publisher, Delhi, 1987.
- Sharma, Ram Nath: *Problems of Philosophy*, Kedar Nath Ram Nath & Co, Meerut, date n.a.
- Sinha, S.P. *Santhal Hul*, p. 33, The Bihar Tribal Welfare Research Institute, Ranchi, 1991.
- Sinha, Aditya Prasad: *Ho Lok-katha*, Vikalp Prakashan, Delhi, 2014.
- Staal, Frits: *Discovering the Vedas*, Penguin, New Delhi, 2008.
- Swami Satya Prakash Saraswati Satyakam Vidyalankar *English translation*, Rigveda——*Vol I –XII*, DAV Publication Division, Delhi, 2011.
- Trigunayat, Jagdish: *Munda Lok-kathayen*, Govt of Bihar, Ranchi, 1968.
- Trigunayat, Jagdish: *Munda Lok-geet*, Bihar Rastra Bhasha Parishad, Second Edition, Patna, 2000.
- Vatsyayan: *History of Western Philosophy*, Kedar Nath Ram Nath & Co, Meerut, date n.a.
- Wansbrough, Henry (Ed): The *New Jerusalem Bible*, Longman and Todd Ltd, London, 1985.